PEACE AFTER ABORTION

309 Smithfield Street STE 210
Pittsburgh PA, 15222
740-963-9565 www.rehumanizeintl.org

PEACE AFTER ABORTION

by

Ava Torre-Bueno, LCSW

PIMPERNEL PRESS
SAN DIEGO, CALIFORNIA

Copyright © 1997 Ava Torre-Bueno. Printed in the United States of America. All rights reserved. No part of this book may be reproduced or transmitted in any form or by any means, electronic or mechanical, including photocopying, recording, or by an information storage and retrieval system—except by a reviewer who may quote brief passages in a review to be printed in a magazine or newspaper—without permission in writing from the publisher. The sole exception is that the meditation on page 148 may be copied. For information, please contact Pimpernel Press, P.O. Box 33110, San Diego, CA 92163-3110.

Diagnostic and Statistical Manual of Mental Disorders, Fourth Edition diagnoses reprinted by permission of The American Psychiatric Association.

PUBLISHER'S NOTES

The ideas, procedures, and suggestions in this book are not intended as a substitute for seeking professional mental health help if needed.

To protect the confidentiality of the individuals involved, all names have been changed, and biographical details have been altered or disguised. In a few cases, stories have been combined to form composites.

"Peace After Abortion" is a registered trademark of Ava Torre-Bueno, LCSW.
Cover design by Paul Hartsuyker, artist and illustrator.
Author photo by Lynn Govea.
Typesetting by Josef Teodorovitch Letsitsky and Kate Mayne.

First edition © 4/96   1000 printed
Second edition © 1/97   4000 printed

Library of Congress Card Catalogue Number: 96-72071.

ISBN: 0-9651383-1-3

ATTENTION FAMILY PLANNING ORGANIZATIONS, COLLEGES AND UNIVERSITIES, AND PROFESSIONAL ORGANIZATIONS: Quantity discounts are available on bulk purchases of this book for educational training purposes, fund raising, or resale to clients. For information contact: Marketing Department, Pimpernel Press, P.O. Box 33110, San Diego, CA 92163-3110, (619)266-8089.

*This book is dedicated to
my generous and resilient mother
Evelyn Torre-Bueno
and to the memories of
my beloved friend Joe Garel
and my quixotic father
Theodore Torre-Bueno.*

TABLE OF CONTENTS

ACKNOWLEDGEMENTS	ix
INTRODUCTION	1
WHY AM I FEELING SO BAD?	7
HOW POST-ABORTION DISTRESS REVEALS ITSELF	21
GUILT	31
GRIEF	55
SHAME	73
DEPRESSION AND ANGER	83
SPIRITUAL INJURY	105
SOMETIMES MEN HAVE TROUBLE WITH ABORTION TOO	115
TALKING ABOUT IT	133
SELF-FORGIVENESS, ATONEMENT, AND RITUAL	141
HEALING INTO THE REST OF YOUR LIFE	157
APPENDIX: HOW PARENTS FEEL	161
CHAPTER NOTES	173
FURTHER READING	177
BIBLIOGRAPHY	179

ACKNOWLEDGEMENTS

It took many people to make this book possible and I want to thank them all. First and foremost I thank my mother Evelyn, my sister-in-law Susi, and my nephew Ted for their constant and loving support; and especially my brother Jose for his support and technical assistance. My friends Dennis Howerton and Rick Avery, LCSW, both told me repeatedly that I had to write this book, and I never would have started without their insistence, or continued without their encouragement. Susan Levine, Ph.D., was invaluable in editing for psychological accuracy, and Ellen Speert, MEd. A.T.R.-B.C., helped me get past the stuck places. Debbie Friedman, my friend since nursery school, engaged in years of discussion with me about abortion ethics, politics, and feelings, and read the manuscript through providing concise editorial comments all along.

Many other friends encouraged and supported me: Polly & Tom, Vivian & John, Judy & Joseph, Jean & Paul, Jean & George, Cathy & Kenneth, and the members of the meditation groups I sit with. My deepest thanks go to the many women and men who have shared their abortion experiences with me, and who have shown me the resilience and hope that lead to deep healing.

Even though I could never have written this book without the help of all these good people, the responsibility for any errors contained herein rests solely with me.

INTRODUCTION

Alicia sat rigid on the edge of the examining table, waiting for the doctor. Her hands were locked around each other, unmoving, and her lips were tight. She was answering my questions with a shake of her head or a one-syllable word. I asked her, "What part of this abortion are you most concerned or worried about?" Her eyes filled with tears. She looked toward the ceiling and wailed, "Can God ever forgive us?"

Who listens to women like Alicia?

Abortion is the most hotly debated political issue of our time. Those who favor legal abortion believe every woman must have control of her fertility from birth control to abortion. Those opposed would deny women this power, and often are as opposed to contraception as they are to abortion. Both sides must present extreme forms of their positions in order to make their points politically.

Pro-choice activists point to the horrors of illegal abortion before 1973 to demonstrate the need for legal, low-cost, easily accessible abortion. Women died by the thousands before 1973 from trying to induce abortions by putting the end of an open coat-hanger into their uterus to dislodge the fetus, or throwing themselves down a flight of stairs, or douching with lye.

Remembering these tragic deaths, pro-choice advocates tend to gloss over the physically, emotionally, and spiritually painful aspects of legal abortion in their political rhetoric, although they acknowledge abortion is a difficult choice that no woman takes lightly.

Anti-choice activists show pictures of second-trimester abortions to shock people into seeing the horror of abortion. Late abortion really does look ghastly, and a mislabeled picture blown up ten times is a distorted but powerful reminder of the real existence of the fetus. Anti-choice advocates make patently false claims about the fetus' ability to feel pain or to know what's happening during an abortion. They highlight the stories of women who are caught in the web of spiritual and emotional suffering after an abortion as proof that abortion hurts all women. Each side has something valid to say to the other, but the political stakes are too high for either side to listen.

Without a voice in the debate are the 3,600 women who have an abortion each day in this country. How did they feel about their abortion experiences? What was it like to find out you were pregnant when you didn't want to be? How did you think and feel your way through the process of deciding what to do? Whom did you talk to—could anyone help without judging? What was it like to be in the clinic or doctor's office? Was your abortion physically painful? How did you feel physically, emotionally, and spiritually two hours, two days, two months, two years, two decades afterwards?

If you picked up this book, chances are you're a woman who is hurting in some way after an abortion. This book is meant especially for you. If you are the partner or parent or friend of a woman who's had an abortion and you're troubled by the experience, this book will be helpful to you, too. It will explore the many reasons women become pregnant at the wrong time for them, and the difficult path toward making the decision to have an abortion.

Distress after an abortion is almost always about another unresolved painful experience in your life. This may not make sense to you right now, but as you explore each chapter of this book, you will probably be surprised to find how connected your feelings about the abortion are to feelings you have about other life events. Very often, finding out you're pregnant, making your decision, or just going to the clinic or doctor's office for an abortion, makes you feel overwhelming anxiety. Then this anxiety stirs up any old anxiety you have pushed away from your awareness. You are then flooded with emotions from another time or event in your life, but you believe these feelings are only about your current situation.

Most of this book is devoted to helping you understand the origin of your emotional and spiritual pain, and suggesting ways to begin letting go of the grief, guilt, rage, or shame you may be feeling. There are exercises in this book to help you work through your painful feelings, a meditation on forgiveness and healing, and suggestions for rituals and atonement you may find helpful in the healing process.

When you begin to work with someone, including the author of a book you're reading, on something as painful as post-abortion feelings, you need to know the person's qualifications and philosophy. If you are opposed to abortion and you've read this far, you know I'm pro-choice. If you're pro-choice, you may not be convinced that I'm really your ally.

I believe passionately that I can be supportive of every woman's right to make her own pregnancy decisions, and still recognize the fact that her decision may cause her significant suffering. While many women do not have emotional or spiritual difficulty after an abortion, I know from twenty years of experience working with women before, during, and after abortions, that many women have more emotional and spiritual pain after abortion than the current research suggests. I worked for five years at Planned Parenthood of San Diego and Riverside Counties as assistant to the director of counseling, and five years as director of counseling. I have escorted women entering clinics through crowds of anti-choice activists, and volunteered in an abortion clinic for eight months assisting women through the procedure. I represented my local chapter of the National Association of Social Workers to the San Diego Coalition for Reproductive Choice for three years, and I have facilitated a support group for abortion clinic staff to help them with the practical and emotional strain of their jobs. Most significantly, throughout this time I have counseled women who have been plagued by emotional distress after their abortions, both in my positions at Planned Parenthood and in my psychotherapy private practice.

The abortion that most dramatically affected my life was my mother's, in 1962, when I was ten years old. After trying for three months to get a safe illegal abortion from a physician, she introduced a thin, blunt object into her uterus to induce labor. She passed the fetus into the toilet several hours later. Within twenty-four hours she fell seriously ill with an infection and was hospitalized for a week.

I was too young to be allowed to visit her in the hospital, and I was convinced that she had died, but I didn't know the cause. When a neighbor mentioned that my mother would be coming home soon, I was astounded and relieved. But things were not right; my mother was depressed and distant for the next year and my family's life was confused, chaotic, and sad.

I learned to "cope" with the sudden and very painful change in my family by pushing my feelings into hiding and taking charge of everything and everyone around me. If there was no order in life, I had to steel myself to take control and create order. Much of my own growth over the last decade has come through healing the injuries caused by this confusing episode in my family's life. When abortion creates suffering for the woman having it, it also causes great pain for those around her.

Finally, I have never been pregnant nor had an abortion. I have a few more years of fertility left, and if I were to accidentally become pregnant, I do not know if I would have the child or an abortion. Like every woman, I can only make that decision when, and if, the time comes.

1

WHY AM I FEELING SO BAD?

Most women feel great relief after an abortion and most of these women continue to feel comfortable with their decision for the rest of their lives. For many, the abortion was an experience of evaluating their beliefs and goals for the first time, and the experience of this review left them feeling more sure, competent, and confident than they had before. Some women recognize that they haven't been living life the way they really want to, and the unplanned pregnancy and abortion are a wake-up call for making important positive changes.

Between one and six percent of women, however, experience long-term depression after an abortion.[1] Seventeen percent experience guilt.[2] Some women know they will be in emotional pain after an abortion. They may want to keep the baby but they are being pressured to have the abortion by their parents or partner, or by economic necessity; women with family incomes under $11,000 are four times more likely to have an abortion than women with family incomes over $25,000.[3] Other women who find themselves in emotional pain after an abortion are completely surprised by these feelings. They believed they were comfortable with their decision but experience sudden, powerful, and disturbing feelings during or just after the procedure.

Jennifer had an abortion about six months after she was married. She and her husband were struggling financially, and it made sense not to add so dramatically to their economic woes. Jennifer was aware that if her husband had been excited about the pregnancy, she would have been very happy to continue it, but she recognized the sense in having an abortion. Having an abortion carried no moral concerns for her, and being pro-choice allowed her to approach it feeling good about herself.

During the procedure she was overwhelmed with a sense of profound loss and the anguish that accompanies loss. She experienced the emptying of her uterus as violent and invasive, and was stunned that she had any of these feelings at all. Jennifer had been completely unaware of any attachment to the baby. After the abortion she became aware that she was angry at her husband, but because the abortion was her choice, she felt it was unfair to be angry at him. She consciously pushed away her feelings by distracting herself with work and social activity. She became depressed and agitated. It was only after she acknowledged how angry she was that the depression began to lift, and she could talk more openly with her husband about the pregnancy and what it had meant to her.

Some women find feelings of grief, regret, anger, shame, guilt, or sinfulness creeping into their lives over the weeks or months following an abortion. Still other women who are sure they feel fine, may be surprised suddenly months or years later by a rush of difficult feelings after an event or situation that reminds them of the abortion.

These are all women who may have been in what therapists call "denial" about their feelings before the abortion. For some, the denial collapses during the procedure, leaving them feeling worse than they did before the abortion. For others, the denial erodes over time as it becomes safer for them to experience difficult feelings. Others hold on to their denial about their feelings for a very long time.

"Denial" is a psychological process that we all engage in to one degree or another to protect ourselves from painful emotions. It is an *unconscious* process—we are completely unaware of the mechanisms we use to hide our feelings so we can remain unaware of them. There are many different ways to "do" denial, which you will see from the women's stories throughout this book. For some women, the denial is to protect themselves from feelings about the abortion itself. But for most women who have difficulty after an abortion, it is their denial of emotions from an *earlier* event that has been disrupted by the anxiety of the abortion. When this denial breaks down, these women feel emotions they have hidden from themselves for years. They inaccurately believe these feelings are just about the abortion.

There is another group of women who experience difficult feelings long after an abortion, but who have *not* been carrying these feelings hidden from themselves for years. These are women for whom life's circumstances since the abortion have changed the meaning of that decision. A woman who felt sure and content with her decision when she was twenty, might reevaluate that decision as she approaches forty and it's clear to her that she will never have a baby. The abortion then becomes a mistake in retrospect, and she may have *new* feelings of regret and grief.

The question for each woman who unexpectedly finds herself in distress after an abortion is, "Why couldn't I know how I was feeling at the time?" The answers to this are very individual, but many fall into broad categories. They start with understanding why and how she got pregnant when she wasn't planning to.

WHY DID I GET PREGNANT WHEN I DID?

It may be clear to you why you got pregnant when you hadn't planned to. You may not have been able to get to the doctor's office or clinic for the pelvic exam you needed for the pill, IUD, or diaphragm. You may not have been able to afford the pill, diaphragm, or condoms and foam. You may have had your method of birth control close at hand, but were swept away by the passions and pleasures of the moment. You may not like sex very much, and so didn't have birth control handy because you didn't intend to have intercourse. You may have been consistently using a method with a high failure rate like rhythm or withdrawal. A small number of women using the pill, the IUD, the diaphragm, or condoms and foam correctly and consistently do still get pregnant; you may know that this happened to you.

Understanding why you got pregnant when you weren't planning to may be very complex. Sometimes there are unconscious reasons women and men have for risking pregnancy. It requires courage to look deeply into the hopes and fears that motivate your most intimate behavior. It is important to keep in mind as you read about unconscious reasons for your behavior that *you really didn't know* what was pushing or leading you to risk pregnancy. Because you didn't know, it is important to resist the impulse to blame yourself for your behavior. We can only take true responsibility for the actions we are aware of. If you realize that you do many things without being aware of them, then you might want to seek help from a counselor to understand yourself better.

Even if you are certain about why you got pregnant, it can be interesting and helpful to investigate the unconscious motivations for pregnancy in the following paragraphs. If you are pregnant as a result of rape or incest, motivation is not the issue, but the following information will still be worth reading.

DID YOU KNOW ABOUT BIRTH CONTROL?

Many young women don't know anything about birth control. This is always hard for adults to believe because there are myths in our culture that kids are very savvy, and that sex education is being taught creatively and well in all our schools. Neither is true. Many teenagers are painfully unaware about the workings of their own bodies, and few know what they need to do to prevent pregnancy or sexually transmitted diseases. Women in their twenties, thirties, and forties may not have all the information they need, or all the resources available to protect themselves. They may believe that they *should* know, and be too embarrassed to ask.

Language barriers may get in the way of receiving birth control information. For Spanish-speaking women the problem may not be as intense as for a woman who speaks Hmong or Urdu, but even women from the most common immigrant groups may not be able to read in their native language. Hearing instructions on the use of a method once while you're at the doctor's office is not adequate preparation for using it correctly. Rural and poor women have very little access to health care in general and to family planning in particular. Most birth control education is provided by the doctor or clinic where you get care. If there is no clinic near you, you won't get the education or the method of birth control you need.

WERE YOU COERCED INTO HAVING SEX?

Many girls are coerced by their boyfriends into having unprotected sex. Girls are socialized to seek and nurture relationships. Boys are socialized to compete and win. The playing field is uneven because many boys are less interested in the relationship aspect and can extract sex from their girlfriends in exchange for staying with them. They say, "If you won't have sex with me it shows you don't love me," or, "If you won't have sex with me, I'll find someone who will."

These are not necessarily terrible kids. They are as much the victims of peer and societal pressure as the girls they are pressuring, but they don't pay the immediate and severe price of an unwanted pregnancy. Most young men are not like this; they may be eager, but they're respectful and appropriate. Unfortunately, a boy who does coerce one girlfriend, is likely to coerce others, and can cause numerous unwanted pregnancies and the pain and confusion that go with them.

WAS THIS HOW YOU GREW UP?

Young women have tremendous pressures in their lives. They are making the transition from girl to woman, and preparing to become more independent from their families. For some, this is a frightening time full of conflict and confusion. Sometimes this conflict over growing up and leaving home may stem from being raised in a family that is too close and connected. If thinking about separation causes too much anxiety, a young woman may become pregnant to create a sense of connectedness with her baby, or to have her family pull even more closely around her for support.

For young women from families that are not close enough—either cool and distant or chaotic—becoming pregnant in their teens may also be a way of creating a needed connection, or an attempt to get their family to provide more warmth. Like denial, these are not conscious trains of thought but a set of deep and powerful emotional motivations that can lead to behavior the woman herself has difficulty explaining. She may say, "I knew all about birth control, so I don't know *why* I couldn't seem to get to the clinic to get the pill."

DID THE STRESS OF A TRANSITION CAUSE YOU NOT TO USE BIRTH CONTROL?

Women at any transition point in their lives are less likely to use birth control. Again, it is frequently unconscious motivations that cause this behavior. At the beginning or end of a relationship a woman may say to herself (consciously or unconsciously), "I'm not having sex now, so I don't need to use contraception." This may come from even more unconscious feelings that using contraception when you're not in a sexual relationship means that you're *looking* for sex—hunting, planning, being a "bad" girl. Toward the end of her fertile years a woman may mistakenly believe she is not as fertile as she used to be and will take more risks. The deeper motivation for this belief may come from the realization that she will never have more (or any) children, and getting pregnant may seem like a way to postpone the natural grief of this realization. The death of someone close is also a transition point. Women may be shocked to find themselves pregnant within a month or two of the death of one of their parents or other important person. In part, grief is so disorienting that much of the pattern of our daily life is forgotten. On a more unconscious level, getting pregnant may be a way to fill the empty place in the heart left by the person who has died.

WITHOUT KNOWING IT, WERE YOU TESTING YOUR RELATIONSHIP?

Occasionally, women get pregnant to test a relationship. Sometimes this is done consciously but most of the time it is quite unconscious. If your partner hasn't wanted to make a firm commitment to your relationship, you may have neglected to use birth control in an unconscious attempt to see if he would take everything more seriously with a baby involved. When he makes it clear that he doesn't want to be a parent, or to marry, or to support you and the baby, a pregnancy you may have wanted may become painfully unwanted.

Men can also test relationships with pregnancy. Your partner may have neglected to "pull out" during intercourse, or to use a condom. He may have sweet-talked you out of putting in your diaphragm or contraceptive sponge to see if pregnancy would encourage you to commit more fully to the relationship.

Finally, I want to reiterate that women and girls do get raped and are victims of incest. While the majority of unplanned pregnancies are not caused by these atrocious acts, rape (including date-rape) and incest, can and do lead to pregnancy.

The following checklist can help you start to look at the factors that may have been at work when you got pregnant. Try to read and respond to these statements with an open mind. Be attentive to the tiniest whispers in your heart. If you feel yourself getting angry at a statement or rushing past it, give yourself a minute to breathe and relax, and then go back to it again.

CHECK THOSE STATEMENTS THAT APPLY TO YOU:

KNOWLEDGE ABOUT ANATOMY, PHYSIOLOGY, BIRTH CONTROL

- ☐ I got pregnant within six months of first becoming sexually active.
- ☐ When I got pregnant, I didn't know much (or anything) about birth control.
- ☐ I thought I was not fertile because I was too young.

☐ I thought that I couldn't get pregnant at certain times of the month, or by having sex in certain positions.

BOYFRIEND PRESSURE

☐ My boyfriend said if I didn't have sex with him it showed I didn't love him.

☐ My boyfriend said that he'd go out with someone else if I didn't have sex with him.

☐ My boyfriend said I was cold and unfeminine if I didn't have sex with him.

LIFE TRANSITIONS

BEGINNING SEXUALITY:

☐ I felt that sex had to be a spontaneous expression of love, and birth control would have made it seem planned.

☐ I felt it was not really OK to be having sex, and if I had gotten birth control it would have been admitting I was doing something wrong.

IN RELATIONSHIPS:

☐ I got pregnant within a few months of starting to see my boyfriend because it was difficult or embarrassing to talk about birth control.

☐ I got pregnant within a few months of starting to see my boyfriend because we had different ideas about how much protection we needed.

☐ My boyfriend and I were arguing a lot when I got pregnant.

- [ ] We were thinking about breaking up when I got pregnant.
- [ ] I had broken up with my boyfriend, but then we got back together and I got pregnant.

After pregnancies:
- [ ] I was breastfeeding and thought I wouldn't get pregnant.
- [ ] I hadn't gotten my period yet and thought I couldn't get pregnant.
- [ ] I had an abortion a few months before becoming pregnant again.

Pre-menopause:
- [ ] I had recently decided not to have more (or any) children.

Menopause:
- [ ] I had started having irregular periods or other signs of menopause, and thought I was less fertile.

Moving:
- [ ] I had gone on vacation and forgotten to take my method of birth control.
- [ ] I was moving and lost track of my method of birth control in the chaos.

Death of loved one:
- [ ] One of my parents, or a sibling, or close friend died shortly before I became pregnant.

A "yes" answer to any of these statements is worth paying attention to. They can help you begin to understand the circumstances in which you got pregnant. Understanding and acknowledging your areas of vulnerability can help lower your risk for a future unwanted pregnancy.

For many women, becoming pregnant when they didn't want to is the most difficult part about having an abortion. They punish themselves by calling themselves names: foolish, stupid, irresponsible, immature. Recognizing that you got pregnant in circumstances in which many women have unintended pregnancies can help you let go of this shame and self-blame. There is a Cognitive Therapy exercise in the chapter on *Depression and Anger* that can help you change the negative messages you are giving yourself about becoming pregnant.

HOW COULD I NOT HAVE KNOWN WHAT I WAS FEELING?

One reason it may have been hard to know how you were feeling at the time of the abortion is that you may not have been able to confront the painful circumstances that led up to the pregnancy. Feeling coerced in a relationship can be humiliating and harmful to your self-esteem; not knowing about how your body works, when everyone else seems to know everything about sex, can also leave you feeling humiliated and stupid. Approaching menopause can be frightening, both because it is a tangible sign of aging, and because it is sometimes accompanied by disturbing changes in your body.

There are other reasons you may not have been in touch with your feelings at the time of the abortion. If you were raised in an emotionally, physically, or sexually abusive family, you may have very little recognition of your feelings at *any* time. Children who are humiliated, beaten, or molested are so traumatized that they may stop feeling altogether just to survive. These are some of the childhood feelings that the anxiety of the abortion can stir up.

The media rarely covers how women feel after an abortion. Research data are published in psychology journals and don't reach most people. If you have never heard of anyone else feeling sad or angry after an abortion, you wouldn't expect to either, and then you might not acknowledge your feelings when they did appear. It would be easy to convince yourself that the distress you were experiencing was from fear of the medical procedure itself and not about your emotional response to it, or to earlier events in your life.

There is also very little discussion or understanding of grief in our culture. We expect people to "get over it and move on," and we tend to think of grief only in relation to a person we knew who died. Actually we grieve a great deal and never recognize it as such: when we move from a house we have lived in and enjoyed; when our child grows up and leaves home; when we realize in middle age that we're not going to get to do all the wonderful things we had hoped to do in our lives—these and many others are all occasions for grief. Choosing to end a pregnancy is also a time for grief. Most women may not feel it is legitimate to grieve after an abortion because the decision to terminate the pregnancy was their choice, or because the fetus was never a person with whom they had a relationship.

Sometimes when we are in conflict we put aside our feelings to make decisions easier for ourselves. If you were caught between wanting to keep your baby, and hurting or disappointing your parents, you might have unconsciously pushed away the feelings of loss and anger you were likely to feel with the abortion. If you were morally opposed to abortion but were simply too poor to give your child a decent life, you might understandably rationalize away your moral qualms for a little while, only to have them return in force sometime after the abortion.

Sometimes the conflict is so great that you can't make a decision, and someone else steps in and makes it for you. If you were this ambivalent about the pregnancy, it would be natural for someone who cared about you to try to give you guidance. Because others can never fully know how we are feeling, guidance like this can often be more hurtful than helpful. If someone else made the decision for you, you may be very unhappy or angry after the abortion.

For some women, the abortion is not really what they are grieving. It was just the key that opened the door to long-buried, unfinished grief for someone they lost long ago. It may not be obvious at first that this is what is happening, but a woman may sense she is being overemotional and recognize that her emotions are out of proportion to how she is really feeling about the abortion.

It may be that I haven't mentioned the reason *you* didn't know how you'd feel after the abortion. We are all so interesting and complex that each woman reading this book is going to have a unique abortion distress to understand and heal. The stories in the next chapters won't be exactly your experience either, but may be similar enough to yours to help you understand and appreciate your own feelings.

2

HOW POST-ABORTION DISTRESS REVEALS ITSELF

When Carrie came to see me she was looking for help with depression and anxiety stirred up from being in a new relationship with a very loving and supportive man. The unfinished terrors created by a physically and emotionally abusive former boyfriend were exploding around her, and she recognized that her feelings might destroy her current healing relationship. She was also confused by the fact that she was not using her diaphragm regularly even though she did not want to become pregnant at this time: her boyfriend was raising his child alone, and early in the relationship told her that he didn't know if he ever wanted more children.

In taking Carrie's history, I asked about life in her family, her academic and work career, health and substance abuse issues, and about her sexual life and pregnancy experiences. Carrie became tearful as she told about two abortions she had had in the previous nine years. She dried her eyes, astonished that she still had such strong feelings about events she thought she had resolved long ago.

After we had spent several weeks beginning to work on the issues which had brought her to therapy originally, Carrie turned the conversation to her abortions. There was no question in her mind that she had made the right choice in both cases. A child would have held her more tightly in the life-threatening relationship with her abusive former boyfriend, and the second pregnancy several years later would not have allowed her to escape from him. She discovered in therapy that she *desperately* wanted to have a baby, and that she had a deep conviction that she would never be able to conceive again.

At the time of her second abortion there was concern that the pregnancy was growing in her fallopian tube. The ultra-sound technician was abusive and unprofessional to her; he said, "It's a shame you're killing this baby instead of accepting the responsibilities of motherhood." The doctor, being careful, said, "It isn't an ectopic pregnancy. You'll *probably* be able to have children in the future." Since then she had felt that there was something very wrong with her for having the abortion, and was convinced that she would not be able to have children when she felt ready to. These feelings were too frightening for her, and Carrie buried them deep inside her.

Her feelings were "forgotten," but they were not gone. Carrie realized that her inability to use her diaphragm was her way of testing her fear that she'd never become pregnant again. She was helping to raise her boyfriend's two-year-old daughter, and this made her even more acutely aware than ever that she had a powerful desire to be a mother. This understanding led to grieving for the two babies she hadn't had. She couldn't grieve for them earlier because she had no one to support her in thinking of them as babies or children she had lost.

In therapy, she could grieve for them for the first time. She also understood that even though she was not religious, she felt damned in some way for having the abortions. Her guilt expressed itself as fear that she'd never be able to conceive again. The doctor who was being overly careful in talking to her about her future fertility had fed into this concern too. As a result of experiencing her difficult feelings, much of Carrie's depression and fear lifted and she was able to use her diaphragm every time she had intercourse; she was no longer compelled to replace the babies she had lost.

Some women, like Carrie, are completely unaware that the emotional pain they are suffering stems from an abortion. Many other women know that the emotional pain they are suffering is a direct result of an abortion even if they are not sure why it is so troubling to them.

Lupe was a 24-year-old woman who came to therapy suffering from a deep clinical depression. She was able to work, but felt none of the previous enjoyment that work had provided her. She had broken up with her boyfriend about six months before but was not dating; except for weekly dinners with her family, she wasn't engaged in any social activity. She felt worthless, tired, anxious, and sad all the time. She had been distressed for a year, and she was fully aware that her feelings were directly related to an abortion she had had a year ago, but she didn't understand why she felt so empty and hopeless.

Lupe was Catholic and from a very conservative parish, but her concerns about the abortion were not about "sin," or taking a human life. The most predominant feeling in her depression was one of guilt for being harmful or dangerous to her boyfriend. This seemed very confusing to her and to me. Was this more accurately guilt about harming the baby? We investigated this deeply but she didn't feel as though she had harmed a real baby. She seemed comfortable that she had made her choice to have an abortion clearly and thoughtfully, and that despite the Church's stance on abortion, she did not feel she had taken a life.

So why did she feel she had harmed her boyfriend? She had never told him she was pregnant or that she had had an abortion. Did she feel she had deceived him, that he was entitled to know about a pregnancy he was part of? This was not her predominant concern although she did sense that she had been unfair to him in not telling. She felt very strongly that continued contact with her would be harmful to him; that she could hurt him in some mysterious and unnamable way.

In the next session I began to take a history of Lupe's life experience. Many therapists take a history early in the therapeutic process in order to have an outline of the life of the client. This can be very helpful in identifying old injuries and pressures on the client that she or he is unaware of, which are fueling the current distress.

Lupe was the youngest child in a large and loving family. Her life was untraumatic in general, and she was confident of the love she experienced from her parents and siblings. Her academic experience was enjoyable and uneventful, and her dating and sexual history was normal and appropriate. When I asked about her family's medical history, Lupe began to tell me about a serious heart attack her father suffered when she was eight years old. Then she began to cry.

She was surprised by her tears and the strength of her feelings, and she tried to calm herself but she couldn't. She became overwhelmed and sobbed for several minutes. When she could talk again she told me what had happened. She came home from school one day to find her family in a state of fear and confusion. Her older sister told her that her father had had a heart attack and gone to the hospital, but Lupe didn't know what that meant, and she thought he had died. She was too young to be able to visit him in the hospital so she couldn't be reassured that he was going to be all right.

Each of her older siblings had a job to do while their father was hospitalized and their mother stayed with him at the hospital. One brother did the shopping and laundry. An older sister cooked and got the younger kids to school in the morning. The middle siblings kept the house dusted and vacuumed, but Lupe wasn't given a chore to do and she felt insignificant and worthless. Her worthlessness became a feeling of being at fault for what had happened—she came to believe that she had caused her father's heart attack.

In telling me this story, which was full of surprising feelings for her, Lupe became aware that the guilt and harmfulness she felt towards her former boyfriend were the painful feelings from her childhood which she had never had an opportunity to talk about, understand and resolve. Much of the rest of her therapy was working with the feelings from her father's heart attack. As she explored the hurt, loneliness, and anger of being left out of the family during its time of crisis, she became less depressed and anxious. Because her depression had been severe and long-lasting, Lupe needed almost a year until she felt she was finished with therapy. In that time she had recovered from the depression, received a promotion at work, and started dating again.

As these two examples show, post-abortion distress can be painfully and immediately obvious to the woman who has just had an abortion, or it can be secret and hidden from her conscious awareness. The suffering caused by abortion can be about many different feelings. Lupe's depression was fueled by guilt and anger at not being included in her family's crisis; Carrie's anxiety and confusing behavior were caused by grief and fear. In addition to depression, guilt, anger, fear, and grief, women experience many other painful or unacceptable feelings after an abortion. These include "excessive" grief, regret, shame, and spiritual injury.

Difficult feelings may not present themselves clearly and directly. A woman may find herself feeling restless or agitated and having difficulty sleeping, but not have any idea about what is troubling her. She might, in fact, be developing serious depression. Another woman might find herself lashing out angrily at those close to her. If she is not usually like this it may be confusing and frightening, but she may have no idea that these angry feelings are associated with her abortion, or with older feelings that the abortion stirred up.

Guilt and grief may both be hidden very deeply. There may be no outward expression of them, except that the woman may be avoiding coming in contact with babies and small children. She may become "blue" or depressed each year around the time of her abortion, or around the time the baby would have been born, but not consciously make the connection between her feelings and the anniversary they mark. On the other hand, a woman may experience grief she considers to be out of proportion to how she felt about the pregnancy. Or she may be confused at feeling "out of control." "Excessive" grief may not be about the abortion at all, but about grief she didn't get to experience when someone close to her died or abandoned her in the past.

Some women experience fear after an abortion. They may not recognize that it is related to the abortion because it may develop slowly. They may become fearful of being harmful to others (like Lupe), become convinced that they will never be able to get pregnant, or they may fear another pregnancy so much that they become afraid of having sex. This fear may look more like a sudden or slow loss of interest in sex.

Shame may also grow over time, but not be consciously associated with the abortion. Shame and guilt are not the same thing. Guilt is the bad feeling of having harmed someone else or done something we know is wrong. Shame is the feeling of *being* wrong; that you are just flawed to the core. Shame may present itself as disabling self-consciousness, or feelings of worthlessness and low self-esteem.

Regret is more direct. Some women feel that they simply made the wrong choice when they had the abortion. They may find themselves being very self-critical and judgmental, and they may become judgmental and harsh towards others. They may blame others for forcing them to have an abortion they never wanted to have. Regret can feel overwhelming because there is no apparent way to ever feel differently.

Isolation is a major component of post-abortion distress. The sense that having an abortion makes her dirty, bad or sinful, can leave a woman isolated in her painful feelings. For most women who are unhappy after an abortion, the unhappiness is a closely guarded secret. Many keep their unhappiness secret even from themselves through the unconscious mechanisms of denial. Secrets have a way of festering and becoming more damaging over time.

Manuela was in a workshop I presented to a group of social workers on *Peace After Abortion*. For the first time in her life she told the story of her abortion. She had become pregnant as a teenager and had an illegal abortion. She had been certain that if her parents found out she was pregnant they would be terribly disappointed in her, so she had an abortion even though she believed it to be a sin.

When she married in her twenties, she was too ashamed of the abortion to tell her husband about it. They had difficulty conceiving a child, and she was convinced that she was being punished by God for having had the abortion. She felt harmful to her husband, because her punishment was now hurting him as well, and she was lying to him by not telling him that it was all her fault. She eventually conceived and had a difficult pregnancy and dangerous childbirth in which she almost died. She took this hardship as proof that she had to pay dearly to make up for her sinfulness.

This woman had suffered absolutely alone for thirty years! She had been burdened with her sense of sinfulness, with feeling that she deserved punishment, and with the belief that God, who could forgive anyone else, would never forgive her.

These short descriptions of the feelings that women can experience after an abortion may have helped you identify what's going on inside you. It may be very clear to you which feeling you've been struggling with and why. Or you may feel confused because it sounds like several of the feelings are troubling you. However your post-abortion distress has manifested itself, you are now in the process of healing. Understanding your feelings is the first step. The next chapters are about the emotions you may be struggling with, and many have exercises to help you work through these feelings. Chapter Nine, *Talking About It*, and Chapter Ten, *Self-Forgiveness, Atonement, and Ritual* contain ideas about how to continue and deepen the healing process.

v

3

GUILT

WHAT IS GUILT?

Guilt is the deep-in-your-gut feeling of having done something wrong. It is an emotion, a feeling in your body. You are especially likely to feel guilty when you have done something that harms someone else. This harm might be physical, emotional or spiritual. Guilt includes anxiety, self-reproach ("I'm a bad person for having done that"), and sometimes the feeling of having stolen something from someone even if you didn't actually take anything. Often, as adults, it takes us a while to realize that the unpleasant feeling we are having is guilt.

Children are very aware of feeling guilty. It is an experience you can remember clearly many years later. Try this: Recall a time when you were little and you didn't take responsibility for something hurtful you had done, and another child was punished instead of you. Try to recall the feelings you had, how you felt when you saw the other kid, maybe your sister or brother, being punished for your misbehavior. Or, remember a time when you were caught in a lie. Stay aware of the feelings that you have in your mind and body as you remember this. Are they similar to the feelings you have been having since the abortion?

As we grow up, we learn ways to avoid some of the pain we feel with guilt. We *intellectualize* and *rationalize* our behavior. These are two of the unconscious ways we defend ourselves from emotions that are too painful to feel. When you intellectualize, you stay far away from feelings. You are only thinking about the abortion but not having any emotions about it. Like all defenses, this is unconscious. You might find yourself doing this consciously too. As a feeling comes up inside you, you might say to yourself, "No, I don't want to deal with that. I'll get busy with something else." When you rationalize, you explain all the reasons for your behavior. You may make up excuses for your behavior after the fact to make yourself feel better. You might do this inside your head or you might talk to others. There's nothing wrong with remembering the reasons you had to have the abortion. It's only a problem if you're unconsciously rationalizing as a way to not feel painful emotions about the abortion.

I'm *not* saying that every woman who's had an abortion and can calmly tell you the reasons for it is intellectualizing or rationalizing. Most women who have abortions aren't plagued by guilt, and so they can remember the abortion without being overwhelmed by painful feelings. You may know that you feel guilty about the abortion, or you may be reading this and thinking "I don't *think* I feel guilty, but what if I'm rationalizing or intellectualizing?"

Read the guided imagery exercise below into a tape recorder or have a friend read it to you. If you are recording it, leave pauses of about five seconds where they are suggested in the exercise by dots (......) so you have time to follow the instructions. Doing this exercise may help you find hidden feelings, or it may help you recognize that you are not intellectualizing or rationalizing away any guilt. Some people take to guided imagery very easily. For others it takes practice. If this exercise is difficult for you, just try it again as often as you like and see if it gets easier. Not everybody can visualize, and some people get anxiety feelings when they start to relax. There's nothing wrong with you if you find it hard or impossible to do this kind of exercise.

EXERCISE

Close your eyes and relax your body by getting into a comfortable position... Pay attention to the places you normally hold tension... your forehead... around your eyes... your jaw. Make sure that your tongue isn't held onto the roof of your mouth. Let your tongue just relax and rest easily in your mouth. Notice the back of your neck and shoulders. If they're tense, take a breath in, and as you breathe out, just let all the tension go out of your shoulders and your neck... Notice your upper back and your chest, letting them relax as you breathe in and out... Pay attention to your arms and hands. Feel where they touch the arm of your chair or the floor and let them soften and melt into the chair... Notice your lower back and belly and let your breath take any tightness away. Notice your hips... your buttocks and your pelvis... breathe in and out and let that part of your body relax. Pay attention to your thighs and the back of your thighs and feel where they make contact with the floor or your chair... Really let those big muscles just loosen and soften and relax. Let your knees and shins soften and your feet relax... Feel your whole body just becoming softer and more relaxed and melt... Melt in your body until it's very soft and relaxed... Now pay attention to your breath.

Breathe in and let your belly rise... Breathe out and feel your belly fall... If only your chest rises and falls when you breathe, you're not getting enough air. Put your right hand on your belly below your belly-button and breathe in so your belly rises and your chest doesn't move very much. This is a way to breathe completely, so you're getting enough oxygen with each breath. It's a more relaxing way to breathe once you get used to it. Breathe this way for one whole minute.

Let your thoughts float away with each out breath...... Now imagine yourself standing at the top of a flight of stairs. See the stairs, the stairway, the handrail. What are these made out of?... Are they made out of wood, metal? What color are they?... What is the light like where you are? Where is it coming from?... Are you outdoors or in?... Is it dark or light?... Put your hand on the handrail and feel in your imagination what that's like under your hand. Is it rough or smooth?... cold or warm? Now with each breath out imagine yourself walking down one step. Count backwards from ten to one as you go down the steps. Take a breath in and out... ten... breath in and out... nine... eight... seven... six... five... four... three... two... one...

Now look around and see where you are. Notice a door. What's it made out of?... What color is it?... Touch the door and feel it under your hand. What does the surface feel like? Find the door handle... what does it feel like? This is the door to a very protected place. There's real safety behind this door. Notice how you are feeling as you get ready to open this door and walk into this very safe place... Open the door, walk in, close the door behind you and stand still... Look around and notice what's there... At first it might be quite foggy and cloudy. But it might not. Just take your time and notice what's there.

Are you indoors or outdoors?... Is it light or dark?... What's around you?... If it's cloudy, just take your time and see if the place around you comes into focus. Walk around this place and notice what's there. Is there furniture?... If it's outdoors, are you by a meadow or stream?... Just pay attention to whatever's there. Stop for a moment and feel the air of this place on your face...... Is it cool or warm, moist or dry?... Take a deep breath in and smell this very safe place. What does it smell like?... Next, find a place to sit comfortably. Make yourself really comfortable in that place... If you would feel cozy being wrapped up, find a blanket in your safe place to wrap yourself in. Whatever you need to feel comfortable and safe, find it in this place and have it with you while you're sitting. Relax, notice your breath, your belly rising and falling, and then imagine that a "being" comes to you in your safe place. This being is wise and intelligent, kind and caring... Whatever form this being takes, it is there to protect you, care about you, and help you understand yourself. When you've gotten used to this being, have a conversation. Talk to him or her or it and say: "I have had an abortion." Let the being ask you questions like, "How do you *feel* about the abortion?" or "What sensations do you notice in your body when you remember the abortion?"

    Really let yourself consider the being's questions. Try not to think up the being's questions or your answers, just let them arise in you as you sit quietly in your safe place breathing easily in and out. Tell the being the answer as you become aware of it... Let the being ask you other questions to help you understand yourself more clearly like, "Do you feel you have harmed someone?" "What kind of harm?" If the feeling of harm is not what comes up inside you, notice what feeling does. Don't try to create feelings of having done harm if they're not there. Keep this conversation going as long as it feels right to you...... When you are done, thank the being and say good-bye in a way that feels right to you... Before you leave your safe place, look around and remember that this is a place you can return to any time you want to...... Open the door, step out and close it behind you. Walk slowly up the stairs. With each in and out breath, count and take a step.

One...... two...... three...... four...... five...... six...... seven...... eight...... nine...... ten. When you're ready, open your eyes.

What was this exercise like for you? Could you see the safe space clearly? Was it easy to imagine the wise and caring being? Could you let questions and answers just arise out of you, or did you feel like you were making them up or forcing certain answers?

So, what did you learn in your safe place? Do you feel that you have harmed someone? If you don't feel you've harmed anyone, read the rest of this chapter anyway to see if anything in it touches you in a way you might not expect. We are all so interesting and complicated that one idea or feeling can be the road into a whole forest of emotions and beliefs we didn't know we had.

FEELING THAT YOU'VE HARMED THE BABY

If you did discover in the exercise that you harmed someone, who is it? Is it the baby? Do you believe you have caused physical pain to the baby or made it feel fearful or confused? Do you feel you have injured the baby spiritually?

If these are the things you are feeling guilty about, it is important for you to have factual information about what the baby can and can't experience inside the uterus. Organizations opposed to abortion tell women that the baby feels pain and suffers emotionally during an abortion. This is simply not true. Physical and emotional distress can't be experienced by the baby before about 26 weeks from the time you got pregnant because the nerve pathways that carry messages to the fetal brain have not finished forming.[1] What we call emotions are the names we learn to give to feelings in the body. Because the nerve pathways that take sensation to the brain don't form until the last third of pregnancy, there is no feeling from the body to experience as emotion and so there can be no emotional pain for the fetus. In addition, learning to call physical experiences the name of an emotion happens in the first three years of a child's life. It is simply not physically possible for the baby to feel pain or emotions.

Even knowing the facts about physical and emotional pain may not help you immediately to feel less guilty about harming your baby. You may be wondering whom to believe about this. It may be important for you to look at the research data for yourself to decide which set of facts to believe.[2] If investigating source material is still not helpful in relieving guilt about having caused your baby physical or emotional harm, you will need to work on forgiveness and atonement. These areas of healing are covered in this chapter and in Chapter Ten, *Self-forgiveness, Atonement, and Ritual*. Even when you believe something intellectually (that the fetus couldn't have felt pain for example), it's your *feeling* of having done harm that's real for you. This is just how humans work; sometimes we can only respond to the non-rational parts of ourselves. Forgiveness, ritual, and atonement speak to our non-rational selves and we can heal well without ever making intellectual sense of our situation.

SPIRITUAL HARM TO THE BABY

Spiritual injury to your baby is a whole different matter. Unlike physical and emotional pain, where science can make a clear statement about the fetus not being able to suffer, spiritual pain is understood differently by various spiritual traditions. More confusing, your pastor or priest may have one idea about what happens spiritually to the baby after an abortion, and a priest in the next parish may have something entirely different to say about it even though he's from the same faith. More importantly, you probably have your own ideas and feelings about the spiritual impact of abortion on the baby; you may never have thought about this consciously before. This may be what came up in your conversation with the wise being in the guided imagery exercise. You may be surprised by spiritual feelings about the baby especially if you're not a religious person.

> The clinic staff was in a swirl. They wanted me to talk to a woman who was there to have an abortion and who wanted to take the products of conception (the fetus) with her when she left the clinic that afternoon. This didn't come up very often in the clinic I volunteered in, and so the staff felt overwhelmed and unprepared; they didn't understand what this woman was thinking or feeling, and they were too afraid to ask.

> Jill was very calm and collected. She had had an abortion at this same clinic about four years before. At that time she had been given the fetus at her request and had gone with her boyfriend to the mountains and buried it under a beautiful tall tree. This had helped her say goodbye to the baby, and let her feel she had done the best she could spiritually in relation to the child she wanted, but could not have at that time. She was in the same situation again, and wanted to perform the same ritual to soften the guilt she felt for not using contraception perfectly, and having to take her baby's life. It was a powerful way for her to take care of the baby's

spirit and give it peace and beauty to dwell in forever.

Jill wasn't religious in the standard sense of the word. She didn't identify with any of the major religions although she had probably been raised in a nominally Christian home. She was someone whose spiritual sense of her self was found in nature, and in being part of a bigger "whole." Burying the fetus was a way to help her baby be part of the "whole" again. We couldn't let Jill take the fetus with her this time because the law has changed about handling body fluids due to concern about HIV infection. I brought Jill the products of conception so she could say goodbye and we determined that if she wanted it, we could release the products to a mortuary which could then give them to her.

Jill wasn't surprised by the spiritual nature of her feelings, but many women who aren't religious are quite surprised by the power an abortion has to tap into forgotten or unknown spiritual longings. If you're surprised by this kind of feeling, this is just another opportunity to know yourself better. How interesting that you didn't realize you had a spiritual aspect to your personality! Why has that part of you been put aside until now? Was spirituality seen in your family as old-fashioned or silly and something to be ashamed of? Was the religion of your childhood rigid and repressive? Did you turn your back on your whole spiritual self to get away from the hurtful shaming? For some women, this is where the guilt about spiritual injury to the baby really fits: it's guilt about having ignored the spiritual/ethical/moral part of your *own* personality. It's about having harmed yourself spiritually. Spiritual injury to yourself will be covered more in Chapter Seven, *Spiritual Injury*.

HARMING YOURSELF PHYSICALLY

You may be feeling guilt about having harmed yourself physically. If you believe that having an abortion can make it difficult for you to have a baby in the future, you may be feeling guilty about harming yourself as well as feeling just plain fearful. Again, if you have heard that abortion hurts your chances of ever getting pregnant in the future, you've been misled. Twenty years of research data show clearly that even repeated abortions in the first third of pregnancy have no effect at all on future pregnancies.[3] The feelings of guilt for having harmed yourself might be feelings about something else.

Sarah came to see me about three months after she had an early abortion. She was confused by feelings of guilt and anger that had surfaced two months after the abortion. She told me the history of her pregnancy; normally she used contraceptive foam and her boyfriend used a condom. This one time she hadn't used foam and the condom broke.

Sarah talked about the process of making her decision; she and Tony had talked about all the reasons they couldn't have a child now. At twenty-one, they felt they were too young. They were not financially self-sufficient although Tony worked two jobs. In fact, they weren't convinced they were going to end up married to each other. Tony was from a Catholic family so he knew from the start that he'd be uncomfortable with the abortion, but he still felt it was the best choice. Sarah was from a half Jewish, half Unitarian family and felt she'd be comfortable with the abortion.

The abortion was routine, and Tony was with her to hold her hand. Sarah's initial feeling was relief because she had been quite ill with morning sickness, and she felt better immediately after the abortion. She said she had felt sad for the next two weeks and felt she had been grieving the possibility of a baby. So far her story was uneventful.

About two months after the abortion, Sarah began to feel guilty. She would cry when she saw babies and would get furious when she saw anti-abortion advertisements on TV. She felt generally depressed and was having trouble doing her school work. She was a college senior and in danger of not being able to graduate.

We talked about guilt and what it felt like in her body. We together defined guilt as the bad feeling of having harmed someone. Who did she feel she had harmed? Sarah was a little embarrassed. "It would be easy to say I felt I'd hurt the baby, but really it's me. I feel I've hurt myself. I worry I won't be able to have children when I want to." She went on to say that she knew this was irrational because she had had an uncomplicated abortion and her post-abortion physical showed her to be healthy. But there it was. She felt she had injured herself permanently.

I asked about her family history and about what else was going on in her life. Her mother had just had a double mastectomy. I wondered aloud at what point her mom had been diagnosed with breast cancer. Sarah's eyes opened wide; her mom had told her about the cancer just at the time she became depressed! Sarah then made many connections to her mother's gynecological history. Her mom had only one child and then had to have a hysterectomy when Sarah was eight. Her mom's sister had also needed a hysterectomy at an early age. Maybe, Sarah mused, she felt she had missed her chance at her one child and she'd lose her uterus before she could ever have another. Sarah said she felt much better and we ended the first session.

Sarah brought Tony with her to the next session so she could have my support in telling him what she had learned so far. He was supportive, but also saddened by his part in the abortion.

When I saw her the third time, Sarah was still feeling sad and guilty. She was discouraged because she had felt so much better after the first two sessions. She was feeling down about her Nana who seemed to be declining. Nana was her father's mother and had always been the most loving and supportive person in her life. Nana had been battling cancer for years and had generally done very well. Now, Sarah had noticed, she was looking tired and old. The doctor had told them that she wasn't responding as well as she had been to her chemotherapy. Sarah was clearly grieving for her grandmother.

When did she first notice her grandmother's decline, I asked. In September. This revelation was more dramatic to Sarah than the one about her mother's cancer. Her hand flew to her heart and she gasped. She had gotten pregnant within days of seeing Nana. A flood of tears started. When she could talk she said, "I've killed my Nana. How horrible for me!" She couldn't shake the feeling that in having the abortion she had killed her grandmother.

Guilt

Sarah felt guilty about everything! Anything that went wrong in anyone's life, Sarah could blame herself for. There were moments when she understood rationally that she had not harmed her grandmother, but then she would again be overwhelmed with guilt for having done harm. As we investigated, we discovered that Sarah felt guilty for Tony's feelings after the abortion, for her mother's cancer, and for her father's unemployment and depression. Her guilt wasn't only about harming herself by having the abortion, it was just how she felt about everything.

What had made Sarah feel so guilty? As we talked about the family she grew up in, it became painfully clear. Her parents had divorced when she was three and her father had essentially abandoned her. Her mother was a fragile, self-centered lawyer who couldn't tolerate any expression of individuality from Sarah. Any need Sarah expressed was met with, "Why are you doing this to me? Are you trying to destroy me?" Every normal childhood need of Sarah's was turned into a source of guilt for trying to destroy her mother. Sarah's mother was also physically abusive. She would beat Sarah into a corner and smash her head against the wall, all the while telling Sarah what a horrible child she was.

How could Sarah have felt anything other than guilty? We have been working for over a year to heal the effects of her severe abuse, and she's more able to see through her guilt now, but it isn't gone. Sarah has worked hard and is beginning to recognize the intense anger she has towards both of her parents. It's slow work because feeling angry at them stirs up more self-punishing guilt, but she is determined to heal herself and create a life in which she can be a far better parent to her children than her parents were to her.

HARMING YOUR PARTNER

Perhaps feeling guilty about causing harm isn't about you or the baby. Some women feel very guilty about having hurt their partner in some way. They may feel, or know, that their husband or boyfriend wanted them to continue the pregnancy and that he is now grieving or feeling guilty. It may be something less clear. Even if the woman hasn't told her partner about her pregnancy and abortion, she may feel that she has injured him spiritually or just treated him unfairly by leaving him out of the decision-making process. Remember Lupe who was feeling so guilty about harming her boyfriend that she stopped seeing him? She had never told him about the abortion. Her feelings of harming him were really old, buried feelings of believing she had caused her father's heart attack when she was little. Ironically, because she didn't talk to her partner about the abortion, she ended up hurting him by leaving him for no apparent reason.

You may be feeling guilty about hurting your husband or boyfriend because you did talk to him about the pregnancy and he wanted to keep the baby. Your decision to have the abortion may have been based on knowing or believing that he wouldn't stay with you through the pregnancy or support you and the baby financially afterwards. Many women choose abortion because they recognize that having a baby is a tremendous emotional and financial undertaking, and they don't want to risk doing it alone. Not every relationship is a strong one, and women I have talked to before their abortions pointed to their partners' unreliability as the reason for the abortion. Even though she feels she did the right thing for herself, and for the relationship, a woman in this situation might still feel guilty for having denied her partner the child he wanted.

Your decision may have been based on knowing clearly for yourself that you were not ready for the hard work of parenthood even with a partner who would be present and supportive. It is hard to do what feels best for yourself in the face of another person's wishes. Women especially are likely to make decisions based on what other important people in their lives want, rather than on what they want themselves. When a woman goes against this common tendency, she can feel guilty and flawed.

If your partner was supportive of your decision to have an abortion, and then is surprised to find himself feeling angry, depressed or grief-stricken, you might feel guilty. You also might find yourself feeling angry, betrayed, and confused. Just like women, men may use the unconscious process of denial to stay unaware of painful feelings. Chapter Eight, *Sometimes Men Have Trouble with Abortion Too,* looks more closely at this.

HARMING YOUR PARENTS

Maybe you feel guilty about having hurt your parents. Even if they didn't know about your pregnancy, you can have powerful feelings about what your parents would have thought and felt about your pregnancy and abortion. You may know that they would be embarrassed or shocked that you had had intercourse, let alone gotten pregnant. You may believe that they would be hurt or sad to know that you had an abortion. It doesn't matter if you're sixteen or thirty-six; how you think your parents feel about an abortion can have a tremendous impact on you.

Fran came to talk to me about her pregnancy before she had an abortion. She was only about five weeks from her last period and she knew she was going to have an abortion, but she was worried about the guilt she would feel afterward.

Fran had no question in her mind about having the abortion. She was embarrassed by the fact that she had had a one-night stand and that she had not insisted on using a condom. Having no relationship with the man who had gotten her pregnant was her first reason for having the abortion. Keeping her sexual life secret from her parents, especially her mother, was the second reason.

She didn't feel guilty as she thought about having the abortion. She was worried that she would feel guilty *after* the abortion. I asked what she thought the guilt would be about. Her mom, she said. If her mom knew she was pregnant, let alone sexually active, she would lay a major guilt-trip on her.

It was surprising to hear this intelligent, mature, twenty-eight year old woman so caught in what she believed her mother would think and feel. I asked her more about this. I found out that she still lived at home and felt guilty at the thought of leaving. Her mom had adopted a number of children and still had toddlers at home. Fran was expected to function as their mother because her mom was emotionally and physically disabled by depression.

As we talked, it became clear that the guilt Fran feared she might feel afterwards was really guilt she was feeling now but it wasn't about the abortion. Fran felt guilty for wanting a different life than her mother had. Getting pregnant had caused her to think seriously about whether she ever wanted to have children. She had always assumed that she would, but now, faced with a real pregnancy of her own, she felt like she had already done all the child-rearing she could stand and maybe she didn't ever want her own kids after all. In wanting a life different than her mom's, she felt she was hurting her mother. This understanding helped her to think more seriously about leaving home and living her own life.

As in Fran's case, guilt about how parents would feel about an abortion is often a reflection of other aspects of the woman's relationship with her parents.

GUILT HELPS US CHANGE AND GROW

Guilt can be a powerful motivation to change things about ourselves we don't like. Guilt feels terrible, and that feeling can make us look realistically and honestly at our lives and behavior toward ourselves and others. It may be that, in examining the guilt you have had since your abortion, you realize that you don't like how you have behaved in relationships with men. Or you may have come to understand that for you, human life begins at conception and any act which ends that life is wrong. You may recognize that how you and your partner have used birth control feels irresponsible and hurtful to you. Your guilt may show you that being secretive or untruthful feels wrong to you, and that you need to work on being honest and forthright.

Whatever you have learned from your guilt can be put to use to change something important about yourself so you don't have to feel guilty like this again.

This kind of change can be very easy or very hard. You might resolve never to have another abortion. It sounds easy, but if you still have difficulty using a method of birth control each time you have sex, you are very likely to get pregnant again and have another abortion. Sometimes the problem is clear; you can't afford birth control or have no transportation to get to a clinic. Sometimes the problem is more complicated; the diaphragm is right next to your bed but your partner refuses to have sex with you if you put it in. Or you're on the pill but you simply cannot remember to take it every day. If you're in an abusive relationship, you have a big problem that needs immediate attention. The pregnancy and abortion are just symptoms of this. If you seem to have a memory block against using your birth control, some other unconscious emotional issues may be at work and you need immediate attention for this too. These are the kinds of problems that can be helped dramatically by talking to a therapist. Chapter Nine, *Talking About It,* has information on how to find a therapist.

Sometimes the change motivated by guilt is about broader issues. The abortion, and feeling like you've harmed yourself, is just a small piece of the picture. You may recognize that the direction your life is going is not comfortable or satisfactory. The guilt may be about wasting your potential in some way and the change may involve leaving a relationship, changing job or career, or changing the role you play in your family. These kinds of major life shifts may need a lot of support and assistance.

If you try to make the change your guilt seems to demand and it goes smoothly and easily, you're in luck! Keep working on becoming your best possible self. If you resolve to make a change and you can't, or it's difficult and you don't know what direction to take, get help. This is what counselors and psychotherapists are for. Getting help isn't a sign of weakness or craziness; getting help shows that you are committed enough to yourself to do whatever it takes to become the person you want to be.

PUNISHMENT ISN'T NECESSARY

You don't need to be punished for whatever aspect of the abortion has made you feel guilty—guilt is its own punishment. What could you possibly do to yourself that would feel worse than the guilt you are struggling with now? Some people believe that their religious tradition demands that they be punished for harming another or themselves. Most religious traditions actually stay away from punishment, and only require a sincere request for forgiveness and some reasonable act of atonement. Atonement is an action you can take to put yourself right with your own moral code, or to put you in harmony or balance with God, or the natural order of things. Atonement is not punishment.

If asking the person you have injured for forgiveness and finding some act to help you atone doesn't sound like enough to free you from your guilt, you need to look carefully at where you got your ideas about guilt, punishment, forgiveness and atonement. Perhaps you had a very critical and unforgiving parent and you learned that no amount of atonement was ever enough to satisfy her or him. You may have "internalized" the beliefs of your critical parent so now you are your own worst critic. "Internalization" is an unconscious process in which we take traits of people important to us into our own personality. We can internalize positive or negative parts of others. Perhaps you were raised in a church that didn't focus on forgiveness and where the pastor really did threaten the congregation with hell and damnation. These are frightening and overwhelming threats to a child, and you may fear them very much even though you've intellectually rejected the punishing religion of your childhood.

EXERCISE

Do the following exercise on forgiveness even if it seems like letting yourself off the hook somehow. Try not to be critical or judgmental of yourself or of this process. This exercise is about apologizing, taking full responsibility for everything you reasonably can about whatever is causing you guilt about the abortion, and asking for forgiveness. It is important as you do this exercise to *only* take responsibility for your own actions and *not* to take responsibility for other people's actions.

Write a letter to whomever it is you feel guilty for harming. It may be the baby, yourself, God, your partner, your parents, your children, or someone else. In the letter, explain all the reasons you had at the time for each action you took. Explain where you feel you made any errors and what you would do differently knowing what you know now. It is likely that you don't feel you made errors and that you would do exactly the same thing again, recognizing that it will cause harm. Take complete responsibility for your own actions, but be very careful not to take responsibility for things that were not in your control.

When you are done with the first part of the letter, read it over and see if there's anything you want to change. Then write the second half of the letter. Apologize for whatever harm you feel you have done. Say you're sorry with as much sincerity and heart as you can. Say you're sorry as many ways as you can think of. Then ask for forgiveness. Read the letter again and make any changes that seem right to you.

Now put the letter away for a week. Each week for as long as you need to, take the letter out and read it. Really try to feel the feelings that go with taking responsibility, apologizing and asking for forgiveness. When you have finished the letter, close your eyes and imagine that the person you are writing to forgives you. Take a few minutes to sit quietly and experience in your body how it feels to be forgiven. This may be very difficult. You may not be able at first to imagine that you can be forgiven. Just keep working at this every week for as long as it takes. Each week, make any changes to the letter that seem right, and put it away.

You don't ever have to send or give this letter to the person it's written to. You might decide that you do want to share the letter with that person, or with someone else if the letter is to the baby or to God. Take a long time to think about sharing the letter. Make sure that you can reasonably expect the other person to hear the letter with compassion and understanding. If you have an abusive partner or parent who you know will be punishing or will use the information in the letter to hurt you in some way, don't share the letter. It isn't necessary to share your letter with anyone for this process to help you heal, it's just a choice you have if you feel it will be helpful.

The most important person you need to receive forgiveness from is yourself. Chapter Ten, *Self-Forgiveness, Atonement, and Ritual*, focuses on the essential work of self-forgiveness.

A WORD ABOUT REGRET

Regret is the wish that you hadn't done what you did. Regret is a fantasy world that lets you have moments—seconds to minutes—of believing that you haven't had the abortion. In those moments, the guilt, sadness, rage and other feelings you are struggling with are gone and you have some relief from emotional or spiritual distress. The fantasy goes something like this: "If only I hadn't had the abortion. I'd be seven months pregnant—showing—and maybe my boyfriend would still be around. We'd be getting ready for a shower and getting a room painted for the baby." Then reality crashes in and you are grieving or feeling guilty all over again.

Regret is your attempt to soothe the pain, but it only prolongs your suffering. It helps to take a very direct approach to regret. Stop yourself as soon as you notice you are going into your fantasy. Say something to yourself like, "But I did have the abortion, I am working to understand why, and I forgive myself for having had the abortion." Let yourself feel the emotions that come with acknowledging that you've had the abortion instead of trying to push them away with another fantasy or distracting thought.

CONCLUSION

Guilt is the most common negative emotional response to abortion. This chapter has covered a lot of ground and you may feel a little overwhelmed. Just read the parts that seem important to you over again in a few days, and do the exercises even if you find yourself wanting to skip them. Guilt is very closely related to having injured yourself spiritually, so read Chapter Seven in conjunction with this one even if you aren't a religious person; spiritual injury and religion don't necessarily have anything to do with each other.

It may seem that all this work isn't making you feel better. Maybe it's even making you feel worse. When you begin to look closely and realistically at what's going on inside you, you're likely to stir up feelings you have been hiding from yourself. This is a process that takes some time and requires bravery. If you feel too overwhelmed, like you just can't keep digging into these feelings, it doesn't mean you're impatient or not brave. You may just need some help with this hard work. See Chapter Nine, *Talking About It*, for ideas on where to start looking for a counselor to help you through this process.

4

GRIEF

Michelle perched on the edge of her chair and wept as she explained why she had come to see me. "I hate that I went through an abortion! I think about it every day."

She was in a relationship with Phil, a man who seemed kind and loving, and who showered Michelle's four year-old son with affection and attention. Michelle's previous relationship had been with an alcoholic man who was emotionally abusive. Phil seemed so much better for her! When she found out she was pregnant, she felt happy and excited. They hadn't planned this pregnancy, but Michelle was sure Phil would be happy too. She suggested he talk over any concerns he might have with his family. Later, she was dismayed to find he was not happy at all, and she was mortified when he told her that his mother, brother, and sisters agreed with him. She couldn't believe he and his family could be so cold. Because she had borne and raised one child in an unsupportive relationship, Michelle knew that she could not go through that again, and she chose to have an abortion. She expected to feel guilt afterward because she was Catholic and she agreed with her church that abortion was taking an innocent human life, but she was not prepared for the depth of grief that immediately followed the procedure.

Michelle cried throughout the abortion and was inconsolable for the rest of the week. Thoughts of her baby flooded her mind every day, and each time she thought of the child, she became uncontrollably tearful. She had to flee to the restroom repeatedly to compose herself and hide her grief from co-workers. She was sure it was a boy—not because she had been tested for this, but because she was already profoundly attached to this baby and certain of her knowledge of him.

She dreamed about him often. He had dark curly hair and brown eyes that looked at her lovingly, without judgment or accusation. He was never quite her baby in the dreams; she would see him abandoned at a football game and wonder where his parents were, or notice him in a stroller left outside a store. In her dreams, Michelle was filled with an intense longing to pick him up and hold him, but she never seemed able to reach him. During the day, each baby or small child she saw filled her with the same intense longing and grief. She could feel deep despair in her heart, but was terrified of expressing it. She felt that if she let herself go, she would never be able to stop crying. Full of grief at the loss of her child, she was unable to grieve.

Grief is a complex and often confusing set of emotions frequently misunderstood and disallowed in our culture. We expect people who are grief-stricken to keep it to themselves and "get over it." We don't want to hear or see that they are still sad or angry or anxious, six months or a year or two years after the death of a loved one.

Other cultures allow much more room for expressing grief. Just think about the evening news. In the Middle-East, when someone is killed in the ongoing conflict between Arabs and Israelis, the mourners are free to wail and cry publicly. In the Italian neighborhood where I grew up, widows dressed in black for the rest of their lives—it was acceptable in their culture to grieve that long. These examples may seem excessive to you, and I am not suggesting they are the right way for you to grieve; they only demonstrate that how we grieve is dictated by our culture. There is really no *wrong* way to feel or express yourself after a loss.

WHAT DOES GRIEF FEEL LIKE?

Grief is different for each person, but some general statements can be made about it. Deep sadness, intense longing for the one you have lost, confusion, emptiness, anxiety, anger, sleeplessness, and poor concentration all are common symptoms of grief. One person's experience of grief may consist mostly of anger and anxiety, while for another it may be felt as terrible sadness. For some, regret and guilt are closely intertwined with grief. Grief comes and goes in waves. At first the waves are very close together and intense. As you work through the process of your grief, the waves become less intense and get further apart.

BEGINNING PHASE

Grief is our reaction to loss. Many people describe the beginning phase of grief as a profound and excruciatingly painful feeling of emptiness. For women who are grieving after an abortion, the emptiness may be felt in the uterus as a hollow ache where the baby was growing in the womb. You may feel the loss as a deep yearning to see or hold your baby, combined with fear about how difficult this would be for you. You may feel overwhelmed and confused and may find your concentration and memory are not working well. You may wish desperately that you hadn't had the abortion so you wouldn't have to experience these tormenting feelings now. It is very easy to lose sight of the many valid, self-protecting reasons you may have had for seeking the abortion.

In the beginning phase of grief, some women feel shocked disbelief, or forget altogether that they have had an abortion. You may unconsciously construct ways of not knowing that you had an abortion, such as continuing to have pregnancy symptoms or fantasizing that you had some other kind of surgery. Or, you may find that even if you never lose sight of the reality of the abortion, grief includes moments of unexpected and shocking recognition that you are no longer pregnant. Or, you may find yourself looking closely at babies to see if you can find yours, or you may avoid babies completely to suppress the painful knowledge that you are no longer pregnant.

WHAT AM I GRIEVING FOR?

The work in this early phase of grief is to acknowledge and understand your loss completely. Honest acknowledgment lets you continue the process of grieving. Yes, you did choose to have an abortion. What exactly have you lost? Is it the baby you wanted and loved? Had you hoped to continue the pregnancy, but finances, or your partner's or parents' feelings, made you change your mind? If you already were emotionally attached to the baby, you may have had some intuitions about your child, perhaps believing it was a girl or boy. Your attachment may have taken the form of thinking about what the baby would look like, what you would name her, or just talking to him quietly when you were alone. On the other hand, your attachment may not have been obvious to you at all. If you knew from the start that you might have an abortion, you may have repressed any feelings for the baby until after the abortion, when they forced their way into conscious awareness for the first time.

If you wanted to continue your pregnancy, but your life circumstances made abortion seem like the only sensible course of action, you may be grieving over several things in addition to your baby. The circumstances that led to your decision may also represent deep and painful losses.

If your partner didn't support the pregnancy, or you don't have a partner, your grief may be about these losses of relationship. Your partner's lack of interest in the pregnancy may make you feel as though you have lost his love or commitment. You may become aware for the first time that he never was committed to you, and this is the only way you could get that message from him clearly. Did your parents disappoint you by refusing to support your pregnancy? You might be feeling abandoned by them at a time you felt you needed them the most.

If you simply couldn't afford to have a baby at this time, you may be mourning your poverty. Being poor deeply restricts your options, and each and every lost opportunity is something to be grieved. Pregnancy and abortion are as much a part of this economic reality as anything else is; as noted earlier, poor women are four times more likely to have an abortion than upper-middle-class and wealthy women. There are many circumstances that lead to the decision to have an abortion. Each may represent a significant loss in addition to or greater than the loss of the baby.

In having the abortion, do you believe you may have lost your last opportunity to have children? You may be mourning because you believe that this was your only chance to have a baby, or the last chance to have another child that you have longed for. Whether or not this is objectively true doesn't matter—it's how you are feeling now, and it leads to grief for the lost possibilities of parenthood. Once you begin grieving for the children you won't have, you may find that the grief expands to include other dreams you've had that haven't been fulfilled. Perhaps you had hoped to complete high school or college by this age, and you know it will have to wait until much later, if ever, until you do. Maybe you had planned to be married or further on your career track by now, and there is no prospect of this happening soon.

If you had wished to be happier, wealthier, or more together by this time in your life, grief for the lost opportunity of this child and future children will tap into your disappointment and grief about these other aspects of your life. Each of these disappointments must be clearly acknowledged and grieved so you can move into the next phase of your life with energy and creativity. It may be that in actively grieving over the possibility of never having a baby, you figure out how you can have a child in the future. In mourning that you are not happy, you may recognize the path you need to take to make your life more satisfying and joyful.

Did you lose part of yourself—your self-image as a nurturing, caring woman, or as someone together and competent? In addition to, or instead of mourning the baby you haven't had, you may be grieving for yourself. Being someone who has had an abortion may be unacceptable to you; you may feel you've lost the nurturing and loving part of yourself, or been untrue to your faith. You may feel older, as though you have been robbed of your youthful innocence by this experience. You may feel you are no longer good or worthy of admiration or respect. These kinds of feelings are all blows to our self-esteem. Grieving for what you feel you've lost of yourself can help you see that you haven't lost it at all, or it can help you begin the work of consciously becoming the person you really want to be.

Sometimes grief is more for what being pregnant meant than it is for the lost baby. Even though you knew you couldn't continue the pregnancy, just knowing you were pregnant may have helped you feel loved and cared about, or loving and connected to another. If you are from a cool and distant family, or are in a relationship with a man who is not emotionally available, the feeling of connection may have soothed and strengthened you emotionally. Losing the connection that gave you that feeling can cause a great deal of grief.

WORKING THROUGH IT

Latisha was tightly wound up as she paced around my office. As we talked about her abortion, she would occasionally begin to cry, but then bite down hard on her lip and shake her head to force the feelings and tears away. She said she didn't know why she had come because there was no point in dwelling on the past.

Why had she come? It had been three months since she'd had a very early abortion. She had kept it a secret, not even telling her boyfriend Darrel she was pregnant. Since then she had been getting angry with the people around her for no apparent reason. She was having difficulty sleeping, and her ability to do her job had suffered a great deal. She had lost interest in having sex with Darrel, and he was becoming angry and frustrated with her. Others had noticed her mood change long before she had, and one co-worker had confronted her about it a week before she came to see me. In that same week she had been waiting outside of the market for her sister when a woman with a tiny infant walked by. Latisha burst into tears at the sight of the baby and had to sit in the car for half an hour before she stopped crying. She had been crying several times a day since then.

As we investigated what it was that had set her to crying, she became angry. *Everything* was wrong! No one had warned her that she might feel sad after the abortion. She began to cry, and then sob, and then she slammed her hand on the arm of her chair in tremendous frustration. She said something in her had died—not the baby, but some part of *her*. She felt enraged and cheated that she hadn't been prepared for any of these feelings.

What had died in her? Latisha was the shining star in her family, the only person to have attended college. Though she had taken a year off to make tuition money, she was returning to the state university in the fall. Everyone was proud of her, and she cherished their respect and admiration. As she talked about this between fits of crying, she became less angry and more thoughtful. She realized that what she felt had died inside her was her honesty and competence. She hadn't told her family about her pregnancy or abortion because she hadn't wanted to disappoint them or give them the opportunity to think less of her. She hadn't told Darrel because she felt that contraception was her responsibility, and she shouldn't burden him with her problems. This session was the first time she had articulated and recognized the complexity of her feelings.

Over the next few weeks Latisha and I discovered just how much she valued her image of herself as honest and totally competent. This image was in conflict with how she was feeling now. She was feeling pathetic and incompetent and this was a source of deep shame to her. To get the understanding she needed would have involved telling Darrel about her incompetence in using birth control. It would also show him that she had been dishonest—another shameful act for her. On the other hand, she was angry at him for not offering to be responsible for birth control.

We worked for several months on the family dynamics that had led her to feel she should be perfect. Ironically, it was her parent's admiration for her abilities that had set her perfectionism in motion. Like many parents, they had always praised her for what she could do, but out of fear of spoiling her, they rarely praised her for just being herself.

Eventually, Latisha was able to tell Darrel about the pregnancy and abortion. He was deeply hurt that she hadn't trusted him to take care of her. He was also disturbed because he was adopted and he identified with the baby. His grief was less complex and much more achingly sad than hers. Latisha brought him to several sessions, and together they sorted out the misconceptions and miscommunications in the relationship which had left Latisha feeling isolated and driven to take care of everything for Darrel.

When she left therapy, Latisha could look at the pregnancy and abortion as an important turning point in her life. The crisis of her sudden grief had forced her to reevaluate her approach to all her relationships, and ultimately strengthened her relationship with Darrel.

Like Latisha, each time you become acutely aware of having had the abortion, you may have a renewed sense of anxiety, sadness, rage, or longing for whatever you are grieving. Each of these eruptions of grief puts you directly in touch with knowing that you feel bereft. Experiencing these feelings over and over gives you repeated opportunities to mourn, and only through allowing yourself to mourn will you heal the grief you feel.

SECOND PHASE

Confronting your feelings like this is the second phase in grieving. Letting yourself experience the pain is the work of the second phase. It is hard to imagine letting yourself deeply experience grief. You may think, "No, I can't do that. I won't be able to stop hurting once I start." You may wish I could offer something else to help you heal. I can't. Grieving is the only thing that heals grief. Unless you have a history of being emotionally fragile, you will be able to withstand and grow from your grief. If you have had psychiatric problems in the past, you may want to seek professional assistance with the process of grieving.

EXERCISE

To begin exploring grief on your own, give yourself some private and quiet time to remember the abortion and ask yourself what you have lost be having the abortion. Don't stop with the first answer that comes to mind, and don't edit out ideas that don't seem real to you at the moment. Write down everything that comes to mind and let those ideas generate others. When you are finished, review your list and notice which items feel the most important to you. Don't judge yourself harshly if you are grieving for yourself, or the end of your relationship with your boyfriend, rather than the baby.

If you are grieving for *someone*, like yourself, your partner, a former relationship, you have a person to hold in mind while you grieve. If you are grieving a *concept*, like Latisha grieving for her self-image as honest and competent, you may need to create an object to hold in your hand while you grieve. This will help to hold in mind what you are grieving, because grieving a concept is more confusing than grieving an individual.

You can draw a picture or make a collage to represent the concept you are grieving (lost innocence, a nurturing sense of self, etc.), or you can hold an object like a well-worn stone and endow it with the concept you are grieving. Then whenever you look at the picture, or hold the stone, you have an *object* to help you stay focused on what you're grieving, not just a vague concept.

It can also be confusing to grieve for the baby you didn't have. There is no person to hold in mind and grieve for. There never was a baby you could see, hold or relate to in a concrete way. You can make it easier to grieve for the baby by making the baby a little more real for yourself. Create a picture or collage about the baby to give you an image of the baby you are grieving for. Or endow a beautiful object, or a worn stone, with your *sense of the baby.*

Make time to sit quietly with the picture you have made, or the object you have chosen. Allow yourself to notice the feelings in your body that come as you hold this representation of the baby. Let yourself have those feelings for as long as you can. Then put the picture or object in a very safe place until you are ready to do this exercise again.

Sometimes it helps to do this exercise several times over several months, because grieving is a long process that changes over time. At first the feelings you have may be intense or surprising, or surprisingly mild. Doing this exercise more than once will keep you in touch with how your grief is changing and resolving itself. It can help you see that feelings do change over time. You can begin to dispel any fears you might have that you'll feel grief-stricken for the rest of your life.

If this loss has revived old, unfinished grief, be creative. Use the art exercise to create an image to let you finish grieving a long-dead parent or friend, or to let you grieve your lost dreams, or a part of *you* that you feel has been lost along the way.

THIRD PHASE

The third phase of grief gives you noticeable relief from your intense and painful feelings. You will notice that you are not thinking about the baby or abortion all the time. You may be surprised by moments of happiness or concentration that you thought you would never have again. There is still grief during this phase; it can come back to you as agonizingly as it did earlier. But there are times in between the grief now; the spaces between moments of grief get longer, and the bursts of grief become less intense. You will find that you are returning to your old self, probably changed permanently in some way, but able to experience your full range of emotions, and able to return to the flow of your normal life.

It is easy to feel guilty at the beginning of this phase of grief. The first time you really enjoy yourself, or laugh out loud, or desire your partner, you may be angry with yourself for having forgotten that you're grieving. This is a time to be as self-loving and self-forgiving as you can. You are in the process of moving into a new phase of your life. It doesn't mean you will forget about the abortion or the baby you have grieved for, but you will be able to think about this experience with much less pain and confusion than you have now. It is not disloyal to the baby to let the emotional pain of grief subside naturally. You can keep the baby with you always in memory by looking at the picture or collage you made in the previous exercise. You can let go of your grief, and still lovingly remember your baby.

ANNIVERSARY GRIEF

You probably will feel grief about this abortion again. Even if you can let yourself grieve fully now, you may find that you have "anniversary grief" later.[1] Some women find themselves feeling sad or agitated a year later during the same month they got pregnant or had their abortion, but don't make the connection to the events of the previous year. Other women are acutely aware of the day they found out they were pregnant, or the day they had the abortion, or the day they would have delivered their baby, and they re-experience the grief of their loss. This is just another opportunity to allow yourself the luxury of your feelings. They won't last forever, and the more you can just sit and notice them, the sooner they will wash through you and be gone.

Even if it has been several (or many) years since your abortion, you may have a pattern of becoming depressed, anxious, sad, angry, or agitated around the time you had the abortion or the time you would have delivered. You may feel that because it was so long ago, there is no point in looking into your grief now. Try to do the previous exercise anyway and see what happens. Long-ignored or hidden feelings can still be appreciated and healed.

There may be other times that this grief surprises you. If you get pregnant again, unfinished feelings from this abortion can be stirred up. You may find yourself overanxious about the baby you are carrying, or about your infant's health and well-being. You may be unexplainably sad during your pregnancy, or around the time in this pregnancy when you had the abortion in your previous pregnancy.

When you experience another loss in your life, like a beloved friend's moving away or the death of a parent, the unfinished grief from this pregnancy may come up again. This regrieving is normal—it is part of the human experience. You may wish you could get over unpleasant feelings once and for all, but in reality we grieve over and over throughout our lives.

"EXCESSIVE" GRIEF

Rebecca had been referred to me by her male psychotherapist because she wanted to see a woman about the startling grief she was experiencing after an early abortion. She was engaged to a warm and loving man, and had discussed with him all the aspects of their finances, plans, and feelings about her pregnancy. They had agreed mutually that abortion was the right decision for them, and he had gone with her and been present during the procedure to provide support and care. She had been anxious about the medical procedure itself, and felt relieved when it was over, but within a week she was feeling tremendous grief. We explored her feelings more deeply, and it was apparent to both of us that she had not been very attached to the pregnancy, nor did she view herself as having lost a baby. She was perfectly comfortable with aborting a six-week fetus. So why was she grieving?

I asked her about losses in her childhood. Had her parents, siblings, or grandparents died when she was young? Were there recent deaths or losses in her life? No, no one had died, Rebecca answered, but then began to cry. Her parents had divorced when she was four. Her father had just left one day and had very little communication with her for several years. She had felt lost, abandoned, and lonely. Her mother was sad and preoccupied, and Rebecca felt somewhat abandoned by her too. The depth of her grief was for the loss of her father.

In reviewing this loss in light of her abortion, she could identify with her father; she too had needed to abandon a child. She also identified with the fetus, who had been abandoned. The deep grief was for her little-child self. It was grieving she had never felt safe expressing as a child, because her mother was also sad and didn't seem able to tolerate her own pain, let alone Rebecca's. She was also grieving the loss of her image of herself as a supreme caregiver, because she had been unable to care for a baby at this time in her life. While her inability to continue being all-giving to those around her caused her grief, her grieving was also a liberation that let her form a more realistic and healthy concept of herself.

Rebecca and her therapist had worked on her feelings of abandonment earlier in her therapy. They had investigated many of the influences her parents' divorce had had on her life, and her sense of health and wholeness had improved dramatically. They had looked deeply into all available aspects of Rebecca's feelings about her father and mother. So why did the abortion stir up so much unfinished grief? While an unintended pregnancy may be a point of crisis in a woman's life, it is also an opportunity to look at experiences in an entirely new light. This is what happened to Rebecca. The abortion created the opportunity for her to begin to forgive her father and to use this forgiveness to begin improving her strained relationship with him.

DELAYED GRIEF

Sometimes it takes years for grief that we've repressed to resurface so we can mourn.

> When I was eighteen, my mother told me and a friend of hers a little bit about her abortion. She had described all her efforts to obtain a safe—though illegal—abortion from a doctor. She could not afford the $1,000 the physician would charge her, so she self-induced at sixteen weeks of pregnancy. After she passed the fetus into the toilet bowl, she looked at it and saw it was a little boy. When she told us this story, I was aghast, and said something cruel to her like, "How could you do something so terrible?" We let it drop and I forgot about it. But I had not *really* forgotten. I didn't think about it *consciously* for years.

One night as I was driving home from a lecture I had given on abortion, I was thinking about my mother's experience in terms of how important it is to keep abortion legal, safe, and accessible to poor women, so they wouldn't have to go through the frightening brush with illness and depression that she did. Suddenly I found myself thinking about my little brother! He was ten years younger than I; at that time he would have been twenty. I became disoriented, and lost control of the car for a moment as I burst into tears at having lost him. I was astounded by my reaction, but I couldn't shake the sadness and longing to have known him. For a week I was sad and tearful and then the feelings subsided. Once in a while I still cry for my mother's distress, and for the little brother I won't ever know.

FINALLY

Your grief is the unique expression of your deepest feelings about your baby, or for the relationship during which you became pregnant, or for other losses this abortion represents or has stirred up for you. Take every opportunity you can to acknowledge and experience your grief fully, and the grieving will heal itself.

5

SHAME

Gina came to me because she felt she had permanently harmed her body by having an abortion three months before. She was calling herself names like "dirty," and "self-destructive." She felt intense guilt for having hurt herself by having the abortion. As we talked it became clear that she knew intellectually that the procedure was safe and that her body was normal now. She was having regular menstrual cycles and no physical symptoms of anything being wrong. No matter how much she told herself she was physically well, she still was filled with the guilty knowledge that she had hurt herself.

I asked Gina if there had ever been another time in her life when she felt like this. She didn't think so, she said, but then she began to look uncomfortable and squirmed around in her chair. She didn't want to tell me what was going on, and she called later in the week and canceled her next session. I didn't hear from her for about two weeks and then she called and made an appointment.

She was very embarrassed by what she felt she had to tell me. First she said she had tried to make the feelings that had come up in our last session just go away, but she couldn't. She thought now that she understood what was troubling her, but just knowing didn't help.

Very slowly Gina told me about a time as a small child when she used to masturbate by putting her fingers in her vagina. Her mother had discovered her doing this and had reacted with horror. She slapped Gina and told her how dirty and disgusting she was, and that she would hurt her insides forever by masturbating. As she told me this memory, Gina cried and wrapped her arms around her knees like a little child comforting herself. She wouldn't look at me, and when we could talk about this, she said she was sure that I would have the same look of horror and disgust she had seen on her mother's face. Her feeling had shifted from guilt to shame, and she was sure that I also thought she was a bad person for having masturbated as a child.

I assured her that I thought masturbation was normal and healthy for children and adults. With this assurance, she could start to look at the episode with her mother in a new light, and recognize that her mother's reaction was dramatic, harsh, and out of proportion to what had happened. This began to give her some relief from her painful self-punishment. Over the next few weeks we investigated the ways that carrying around this shame her whole life had affected her. We discovered that she had had difficulty using birth control, because it too was tied in with her feelings of guilt for hurting herself and shame for being flawed.

Shame feels close to, but is different from guilt. While guilt is about feeling that you have hurt someone, or have broken a rule, shame is about feeling inferior. Guilt involves some action that you took. Shame involves feelings about yourself.

Shame strikes when you are reminded that you have failed. The feeling in your body may be one of collapsing inside and the intense wish to hide from the sight of others. Even when there is no one else around, you may have an imaginary "audience" judging you that you want to escape from. This painful experience is the collapse of self-esteem. You feel worthless and stupid.

For Gina, the imaginary audience was the memory of her mother's disgusted face. Whenever Gina felt sexual, she was confronted, consciously or unconsciously, by her mother's look of shock and horror. She then felt worthless and flawed to the core. Feeling this way made it hard for her to protect herself in sexual situations, and she frequently had intercourse without using birth control. She left herself vulnerable to unplanned pregnancies, sexually transmitted diseases and HIV, and then felt even more shame for being so incompetent at taking care of herself.

Shame has many other faces. Embarrassment, humiliation, self-consciousness, self-disgust, stigma, and mortification are the most common. For those women who have shame after an abortion, humiliation is often the form of shame they experience.

Humiliation is the feeling of having been forced into an inferior position. There is someone else involved and the other person has more power. There is a loss of dignity and self-worth. Often, the reaction to being humiliated is rage, but if the other person involved does have more power, the rage feels impotent and leads to further feelings of humiliation and shame. A person who has experienced several painful humiliations may start to think of herself as a wimp, the kind of person who can't stand up for herself and who deserves to be put down by others.

Michelle, who we met in the chapter on grief, also suffered from terrible humiliation. She was a practicing Catholic who believed that abortion was the taking of an innocent human life, and yet she had had an abortion when her boyfriend insisted on it. He had said that he wouldn't be able to stay in the relationship if she had the baby, but that he knew they could be happy together if she had an abortion. Michelle felt she had to choose between her own need for security and love, and the baby's need for life and care. Because she had already raised one child alone and couldn't face doing it again, she felt forced into having the abortion.

Michelle felt guilty for having chosen herself above the baby, and felt deep humiliation at not being a strong enough person to do what she knew was right. She related this weakness to other times in her life when she felt victimized and too powerless to protest. She had been molested by her cousin and by a school teacher, and had never felt strong enough to follow through with prosecuting them. These events left her feeling flawed and pathetic, and the abortion confirmed for her that she was a powerless, shameful person.

It would be nice to say that Michelle had worked through this part of her problem as successfully as she had confronted her grief. Sometimes though, things don't turn out so well. In this case, Michelle wasn't ready emotionally to work on the role shame played in her life, and I wasn't able to engage her curiosity and energy for this job. Perhaps another therapist would have been more successful, or perhaps Michelle just needed time to get ready to face this painful aspect of herself. She got pregnant again by the same man and they got married and had the baby. She came back to therapy a few times after that and was feeling humiliated by her husband's apparent lack of interest in the relationship. Here she was in another powerless position! She only came for a few visits and then stopped. When I saw her briefly a year later she was divorcing her husband because he had been unfaithful to her.

Stigma is the other common shame experience for women who have had an abortion. Even though abortion has been legal in the United States for over twenty years, the stigma attached to it has not decreased. In fact, it has increased in the last fifteen years under the barrage of the religious right. Some women who have had an abortion feel secretly marked or tainted, as though they had a blemish of character that others would be repelled by if they knew about it.

Radical anti-choice activists stigmatize women who have had abortions by branding them murderers and sinners. One anti-choice researcher has published research on something she calls "Postabortion Syndrome."[1] She implies that most women who have abortions are traumatized by the medical procedure itself, and will re-experience this trauma in flashbacks and nightmares. She goes on to state that these women become constricted in their ability to express emotion, have difficulty in relationships and can become cold, unloving, and depressed. This research may not intend to stigmatize women who have had abortions, but it has the powerful potential to do just that. Other research, and the clinical experience of therapists, does not support the idea that women are traumatized by the abortion procedure itself. In twenty years of counseling women after abortions, I have *never* seen a client who met the definition for "Post-Abortion Syndrome."

Pro-choice activists inadvertently stigmatize the ten percent of women who have long-term emotional or spiritual difficulty after abortion by denying that post-abortion difficulties exist. For the most part, this is out of their own need not to see the pain their work causes some women. Those women who do struggle with guilt, grief and the other feelings discussed so far, are left feeling isolated and crazy.

Althea felt stigmatized by her abortion. She was sure everyone could see that she had had an abortion just by looking at her face. She often found herself wondering what her family and friends would think of her if they ever found out she had had an abortion. She was sure they would think she was less than human, a blight on society.

In the first few sessions it became clear that if Althea were in the same situation again, she'd make the same choice. She was seventeen and nearing the end of high school. She felt strongly that she didn't want the life her older sister had—a single mom struggling on welfare and frustrated by not being able to get a job that would let her support her son. Some of Althea's concern about what others would think came from her Christian upbringing, and her involvement in the life of her church, but for the most part her religious convictions were comforting and helpful to her at this time. She had prayed for forgiveness and felt it had been granted.

Why did she feel less than human? It was hard to understand the source of her sense of stigmatization. We spent some time exploring for other events in her life that might have made her feel this way, but she couldn't remember any specific incidents. Then she became very quiet and looked agonizingly uncomfortable. She began to cry and said, "It's being black." Then she cried for fifteen minutes. Her crying was alternately pitiful and full of rage.

When she relaxed she began to tell me about each moment of racism she had ever encountered. There were many. She had grown up in an integrated community and had been called names by a few of the kids there. She had a teacher who refused to acknowledge her writing talent but admired a less gifted white child. She grew up seeing few black faces on television and those that were there were only comedians. She realized that the only two ways she ever felt were stigmatized or invisible.

Why hadn't Althea made this connection when we first explored other stigmatizing events in her life? To survive with some amount of self-esteem, she had repressed out of consciousness her knowledge of how bad it sometimes felt to be black in a white culture. Then it all erupted at once. Her sadness was for the hurts she had received just because she looked "different" to some of the kids in her neighborhood. The anger she felt was against the injustice of being judged for something she had no control over. In fact, she was proud of her African-American heritage, and so these surprising feelings of shame created even more shame for her.

Althea wasn't sure I could help her with this. She needed to know if I had any idea of what she was talking about. I told her about growing up in a non-Hispanic neighborhood with an Hispanic name, and that I occasionally had experienced racism on that account. I knew how soul crushing it felt but I certainly hadn't been tormented frequently as she had been. She thought I could begin to understand her with my background and we continued to work together. It didn't take long for Althea to recognize that the feelings of stigma were not really how she felt about herself, but were the "internalized" views of an often racist society. She understood that these feelings would be hard to weed out of herself, but felt that now she knew they were there, she would be able to recognize and reject them. We worked together on this for a few months and then she felt solid enough in her battle against stigma to end therapy.

Healing from shame is hard work. If you were raised in a family where you were called names and laughed at, beaten or molested, you may be living with shame every day. You may feel flawed and deficient to your core. You probably will need help to heal from this kind of shame. Find a therapist you trust and give yourself the gift of his or her care and assistance to help you learn to like yourself. If you were raised in poverty or were stigmatized because of how you look, sound, or act, therapy can help, but it is even more important to recognize that the society that stigmatized you is itself sick with hatred.

If your shame seems to be about the abortion only, work with the self-forgiveness meditation in Chapter Ten of this book.

If you are still feeling shameful in a few months, then seek help from a therapist.

Shame, embarrassment, humiliation, self-consciousness, stigma and mortification are some of the most painful feelings we ever have to deal with. They are not as common in women having trouble after an abortion as depression and guilt, but when they are present, they are agony. If you have felt this way about your abortion, be kind to yourself and do self-forgiveness exercises even if you don't feel forgivable. Talk to someone else about your feelings so they don't remain a secret. See Chapter Nine, *Talking About It*, for the reasons not to keep your abortion a secret, and for ways to start talking about your abortion and your shame.

6

DEPRESSION AND ANGER

This chapter is about the illness of depression and the different kinds of therapy that can help to heal it. Because I am describing theories about why people become depressed, you may find some of this chapter a little technical. It starts though, with a client I am still seeing.

Leah had had two abortions four years apart. I was seeing her five years later for other concerns, when her feelings about these abortions resurfaced. She had coped well after the first abortion even though she was disappointed with her partner for not wanting to continue the pregnancy. The second abortion was with another partner and Leah found herself in the same position she had been in a few years before.

After the second abortion Leah lost enjoyment in everything that usually interested her. She had a hard time working. She often called in sick and stayed in bed all day even though she had no physical illness. She completely lost control of her finances. She couldn't keep track of where her money went because she began shopping compulsively to try to feel better. In addition to her other bills, she ended up owing the IRS a great deal of money. Nothing gave Leah pleasure; she felt worthless and sad, and worst of all, she just couldn't think clearly or concentrate on anything. She found it difficult and unsatisfying to read or watch movies. This period in her life seems hazy and unclear to her now.

In therapy, Leah could see that she had become quite depressed after the second abortion. She hadn't had an explanation for feeling so out-of-balance before. Just having her symptoms named and explained by me, gave her a sense of something solid to hold on to. As she got more comfortable with the idea of depression, that it was an illness we could treat together, she was able to piece together the emotional events that had led to her depression.

Leah knew she couldn't continue either of the pregnancies. She was raising her six year old daughter by herself when she became pregnant the second time. At first she only remembered feeling resigned to having the abortions, but as we talked more, Leah remembered that for a few days, she had been furious at her partner for not wanting to stay with her and raise the baby. Over the course of several weeks in her therapy, Leah came to understand that the rage at her boyfriend was itself a cover for deep feelings of the despair of abandonment. These feelings had needed to be covered up because they were a painful reminder of her parents' divorce and the agonizing feeling of having been abandoned by her father when she was four years old. Leah's mother couldn't tolerate Leah's anger or her despair at losing her father. Because her step-father or mother would beat her if she was angry, it was safer for Leah to become unaware of her anger.

One theory (psychoanalytic) about depression, is that it is the result of turning anger inward on oneself. Another theory (self psychology) says that we get depressed when we are ignored or emotionally injured by others' unattuned, unempathic reactions to us. Leah falls into both these categories. Since the abandonment felt too painful for Leah, and the anger covering it up felt too dangerous, Leah had become severely depressed. In some ways her depression had run its course before she had come to see me, but it had left her with a mild, long-standing depressive illness (dysthymia) that she just accepted as how her life was. A third theory (cognitive) explains part of why Leah remained mildly depressed. With her self-esteem so badly injured, she continuously thought the worst about herself. These thoughts caused her mood to stay depressed.

Depression is a physical illness that changes the biochemistry of the brain. It affects many jobs the brain does. Interestingly, this illness can be brought on by emotional distress, and can often be alleviated by talking about the distress. In Leah's case, the depression was brought on by the distress of two pregnancies in unsupportive relationships. Sometimes the distress that leads to depression is much less obvious. For example, growing up in a family where you are constantly ignored or disappointed by your parents and siblings can leave you ill with depression. Depression can also be genetic; it appears that depression runs strongly through some families.

The important thing to keep in mind is that depression is an *illness of the body*. The organ it affects is the brain. It's like diabetes or any other illness of the body that affects one organ. Just like diabetes, depression is a potentially fatal illness that demands treatment. If your pancreas stopped working correctly, your blood sugar would go up and you'd need to go on insulin to correct the chemical imbalance in your body. If you didn't, you could ultimately die from the complications of diabetes. If the chemistry of your brain is altered by the illness of depression, you need treatment—therapy or medication or both—to get the brain chemistry back to normal. If you don't treat depression it may go away on its own, but it will probably come back in the future. If it doesn't go away, you could ultimately die from the complication of depression called suicide.

I stress the point about depression being an illness because there is still a powerful myth in our culture that people who are depressed are just being lazy, or feeling sorry for themselves, or trying to get attention. You may feel that way about yourself if you're depressed. This is because depression affects the way your brain works, and your judgment, thinking, memory and insight can all be badly confused.

Therapists decide if a person is depressed by noting if she or he has several symptoms of depression but has no underlying physical condition that might look like depression (like having a low thyroid problem). In the *Diagnostic and Statistical Manual of Mental Disorders—Fourth Edition* (DSM-IV), a major depressive episode has at least five of the following symptoms during a two-week period. At least one of the symptoms must be one of the first two, (1) depressed mood, or (2) loss of interest or pleasure.

> Depressed mood most of the day, nearly every day, as felt by the depressed person or noticed by others
>
> Noticeable loss of pleasure in all, or almost all, activities, most of the day, nearly every day, as noticed by the depressed person or as noticed by others

Significant weight loss or weight gain when not dieting, or decrease or increase in appetite nearly every day

Insomnia or sleeping too much nearly every day

Physical agitation or slowing down nearly every day which can be noticed by others

Fatigue or loss of energy nearly every day

Feelings of worthlessness, or excessive or inappropriate guilt nearly every day

Lessened ability to think or concentrate, or indecisiveness nearly every day

Recurrent thoughts of death, recurrent suicidal ideas without a specific plan, a specific plan for committing suicide, or a suicide attempt.

Another depressive illness is called dysthymia, and it is a long-term slightly depressed state. In the DSM-IV, dysthymia is defined as a depressed mood, most of the day, more days than not, for at least two years. While a person suffers from dysthymia, at least two of the following symptoms must be present: poor appetite or overeating, sleeping a lot or a little, low energy or fatigue, low self-esteem, poor concentration or difficulty making decisions, and feeling hopeless. These definitions seem very mechanical and you may not be sure they apply to you. If you suspect you are depressed, think about, and do, the exercises in this chapter. If you decide you may be depressed, and if the exercises don't help you feel better soon, then get professional help with your depression.

NOTE: Most people who are depressed are not suicidal but their lives are full of suffering. They feel worthless and hopeless. Often, like Leah, they get no pleasure from the activities they used to enjoy, and they are oppressed by specific and vague feelings of guilt. Thinking, memory, and concentration are all affected so the person feels stupid and forgetful. **However, if you are having suicidal thoughts or have a plan to kill yourself, you must get help from a professional counselor right now.** If there is a 24 hour crisis hotline in your community call it right now. If not, find a counselor who can see you immediately. If you can't find one, go to a hospital emergency room and tell them you are suicidal. (See Chapter Nine, *Talking About It,* for help in finding a counselor.)

There are different theories on how to treat the illness of depression based on beliefs about how depression begins. Cognitive therapy starts from the belief that the thoughts you think influence your mood. For example, if it's a dark and stormy night and someone you love is late coming home, you may start thinking thoughts about their car going off the road, and that they are lying injured in a ditch with no help in sight. While thinking these thoughts you get more and more distressed. When your friend comes home you may be angry at them for having made you worry, but you're also relieved to have them home. All the feelings that happened—fear, anxiety, sadness, anger, and relief, were the result of what you were thinking, not the result of the actual events that were happening. If you had thought, "I guess he just pulled off the road to wait for the weather to clear," how different your feelings would be!

Psychodynamic therapies look at depression differently. Classical psychoanalytic theory says that depression is instinctual rage turned against the self, because it's too dangerous for a tiny child to turn it against his/her parents. Newer psychodynamic theories like Self Psychology, suggest that depression is one response to having had our feelings and heart-felt concerns ignored or dismissed by our caregivers when we were little, and not being able to soothe ourselves from this hurt.[1]

The medical explanation for depression is that the biochemistry of the brain has been altered in a way that doesn't allow the brain to work well. Whichever theory makes sense to you about what starts depression, once it is started, it becomes a physical, biochemical illness, and if it's serious enough or lasts long enough, it needs to be treated with medication.

COGNITIVE THERAPY

Talking therapies can treat less serious depression without medication. Cognitive therapy works by having the therapist help you tune in to the thoughts you are thinking. It can be surprising when you start paying attention to your thoughts to notice just how negative they really are. You may believe that you're not thinking negatively, and then with guidance in listening to your thoughts you may discover that over and over again every day you're saying things to yourself like, "I can't do this," "This is hopeless," "I'll never be able to get this done right," "Why did I even get out of bed this morning?" Sometimes, if you're more depressed, you might hear yourself saying, "I wish I wouldn't wake up in the morning," or "I wish I'd never been born." If you're severely depressed, the thoughts that are going on inside your head may be, "I wish I could die," "I think I'll kill myself."

After teaching you to tune into the thoughts in your head, the cognitive therapist may work with you on seeing what patterns of negative thoughts you have. Together, you create exercises to stop those patterns of thinking and replace them with more realistic, more positive, more self-affirming thoughts.

This style of therapy may work quickly to alleviate many of the symptoms of depression. With the help of several excellent self-help books on cognitive therapy, you can do much of this work on your own. This is very helpful because most people don't have the money or adequate health insurance to pay for seeing a therapist privately.

Here is a Cognitive Therapy exercise to give you a flavor of how this form of therapy works.

EXERCISE:

For the next two or three days carry paper and a pen with you. When you hear yourself thinking about the abortion, write down every word you use to describe yourself and your behavior. Are they negative, harsh, and self-blaming? List them down the left side of a piece of paper: "I was stupid not to use birth control." "I was selfish and thoughtless to have the abortion without telling my boyfriend."

Now imagine that you are talking to a friend of yours whom you like and respect very much. Imagine she is telling you about *her* abortion. What would you say to her under the circumstances?

On the right side of your paper, write what you would say to this trusted and admired friend. It will probably be a more realistic and forgiving statement. It might go something like, "You say you weren't planning on having sex, it just seemed to happen. This happens to lots of women, so you're not unique—only human. You can learn and grow from this experience and protect yourself better in the future." Or, "You weren't thoughtless; you say you were worried about stressing your boyfriend out because he was in the middle of his final exams. That's very thoughtful. You can still tell him about it if that feels important to you. Maybe if this happens in the future, you can resolve to tell your boyfriend so he can take care of his own emotional needs."

Now go through these statements and change "you" to "I." Read these over so you are talking to yourself in a more forgiving and rational way. Do this exercise any time you hear yourself being harsh and critical to yourself.

While this may seem mechanical, and it may be hard at first to come up with a nonjudgmental phrase to counter your self-punishment, it is very worthwhile. What you say to yourself inside your head is almost always more harsh and hurtful than what your friends or family would say to you, or what you would say to a friend in the same situation. Changing those internal negative messages can change your mood substantially.

Work with this cognitive exercise and see if you are feeling better in a few weeks. If you aren't feeling less depressed, you may need to seek professional help. If you are feeling suicidal, get help right now.

PSYCHODYNAMIC THERAPIES

Psychodynamic therapies look at the historical roots of your feelings and can help you make significant life changes. In Leah's case, the historical roots of her post-abortion depression lay in her parents' divorce when she was a little girl, and her experience of this as being abandoned by her father. She couldn't show her hurt feelings because her mother wouldn't tolerate them. She also had to repress her angry feelings because her mom and step-dad would beat her for displays of anger. As a result of growing up in her family, Leah generally had no idea what she was feeling. She often felt confused and overwhelmed but didn't know why.

Psychodynamic therapy helped uncover the painful feelings Leah had repressed for so many years. After grieving for the unhappiness of her childhood, she could naturally and automatically respond more healthfully to things that used to be difficult for her. She came to know what she was feeling at the moment she was feeling it, and could respond appropriately. She was no longer confused and overwhelmed.

The psychodynamic therapies can take a long time. It can take several months to sort out a specific problem, and several-to-many years if you have a serious history of being abused and injured emotionally. Leah and I have been working together for almost two years.

Psychodynamic therapies cost a lot. Psychotherapists are highly trained professionals, and like other professional healers, therapists are paid quite well. Many therapists will slide their fees to see a few low-income clients, but generally psychotherapy isn't available to poor and working people except in community based clinics. Not every community has a mental health clinic, and so many people have difficulty in finding the care they need. Despite the limits to access, psychodynamic therapies are well worth the time and effort if you want to make significant life changes.

PSYCHOANALYTIC THERAPY

Classical psychoanalysis says that depression is anger turned on the self. You will find that when you are aware of feeling angry, you don't feel depressed. Practice getting angry at someone or something that isn't close at hand, and see if you feel more energized and less depressed. Of course, you can't stomp around all day in a rage, but it helps to really have the physical experience of feeling the depression vanish as you get angry.

Heidi had been depressed since childhood. She came to see me about feeling addicted to an unsatisfying relationship. We worked together for several years and I still see her at times when she's feeling fragile or confused. Heidi had had an abortion about two years before she came to therapy. It wasn't the cause of her depression and she was quite comfortable with her reasons for having it and with the outcome. However, the abortion was somewhat distressing because the doctor was cool and abrupt, and she had needed the procedure repeated because the first abortion was incomplete. This is a very rare complication of abortion.[2]

Heidi noticed that as she told me the story of her abortion, she became less depressed. She was still angry at the doctor for not listening to her when she described her symptoms, and for dismissing her concerns. Recognizing that her anger and her depression couldn't exist at the same time was a revelation. As we worked together, this information helped us track down the deep roots of Heidi's long-standing depression.

Her family was cool and disconnected. Her mother in particular couldn't provide loving care for her children, and Heidi frequently felt disconnected from the life around her, and very lonely. She felt unloved and unwanted. Her father was also distant but less critical than her mother. Heidi remembered as a young child becoming so filled with rage that she inadvertently killed her pet rabbit. After that, her rage was a source of tremendous shame and guilt for her.

Because she had learned as a child that her rage could kill, Heidi had developed a personality style which was based on not knowing how angry, anxious and sad she was feeling. She tended to blame others for whatever went wrong, and to feel entitled to special treatment at work and in her family. She was completely surprised when she was fired from her job, and blamed the "bureaucracy" at work for having it in for her because she was "honest and spoke her mind."

Her long-standing depression and sense of entitlement came from being enraged at the painful treatment she had received as a child. People "owed" her because she had suffered so much. She was depressed because she couldn't tolerate knowing any of these angry feelings consciously.

Our work together focused on Heidi's anger. For a long time she was unable to acknowledge that she was angry at all. She would complain bitterly about her mother or a work situation, but when I asked her what emotions she was aware of, she couldn't tell me. Sometimes, when she started to get angry as she talked, she would become confused and disoriented and then sink more deeply into depression.

This is why psychodynamic therapy takes a long time. Heidi and I spent almost a year working once a week to let her be more comfortable with the feelings of anger she was carrying around. Then she spent a year feeling enraged most of the time. She avoided her parents because she didn't want to make the suffering in her family any worse than it already was. A crisis in her last year of therapy led Heidi to tell her parents about her depression and the family dynamics that had contributed to it.

Her real honesty let the whole family get a little closer and more caring. Many people fear finding out how they really feel because they're afraid it will destroy their relationships with the important people in their lives. Chapter Nine, *Talking About It,* addresses this concern in some detail.

If you don't feel that repressed anger is the source of your depression, answer the following questions:

> Was I sexually abused as a child?
>
> Was I physically abused? (Anything other than a spanking on the bottom now and then.)
>
> Was I emotionally abused? (Called names like "stupid," "rotten," "good for nothing," or worse.)
>
> Was I neglected? Do I remember feeling lonely as a kid? Was I ignored and not paid attention to?
>
> Was one of my sisters or brothers favored over me? Did I always count for less in my family?
>
> Was I abandoned? Did my parents divorce?
>
> Did someone close to me die when I was young?
>
> Was I raised in poverty? Did my family lack basic necessities sometimes?

These are some of the significant life events that usually lead to profound feelings of anger. If you were allowed to experience your anger at the time of the events, you are less likely to get depressed later in life. Many of these experiences happen in families where anger is not acceptable. If this was the case in your family, you may be more susceptible to depression now. If one or more of these happened to you, and if you don't think you've ever felt angry about them, you might want to keep an open mind and investigate your feelings again.

In Leah's case it is easy to see why she repressed her anger out of consciousness. Her mother and step-father were physically abusive to her when she expressed anger. Not knowing she was angry was a survival tool. Not knowing how she felt allowed her to tolerate life in her family.

It may be less clear why Heidi needed to repress her anger. No one was beating her and she hadn't lost a parent through divorce as Leah had. Her parents were "just" neglectful and critical. Heidi felt that her younger brother was favored by her mother. Heidi learned not to express the anger that grew out of neglect, because her mother would get angry in return and ignore her more after each expression of rage. Even when Heidi began drinking in junior high and flunking classes, her mother refused to acknowledge that anything was wrong in the family. Her mom even ignored it when Heidi attempted suicide as a junior in college! Her father and brother came to her aide, but her mother acted as though nothing had happened. Injuries to the self do not have to be physical to be damaging. Heidi's experience over and over again was that she was unimportant and uncared for.

If, like Heidi, you do not always know what you are feeling, try doing the following exercise. It is designed to help you identify angry feelings. Just being able to identify what anger feels like in your body is an important first step to being able to tolerate those feelings and then let them go.

EXERCISE

Start by lying or sitting comfortably with your eyes closed. Breathe in and out slowly and deeply for about two minutes, and use this time to notice if there is tension in your body. As you breathe in, imagine you are breathing into the tense area. As you breathe out, imagine the tension flowing out of you with your breath and feel your muscles relax in that area. Do this throughout your body until you are completely relaxed.

Think of a situation that makes you angry. Pick a situation that is *not* associated with your abortion or with your family so it won't be too overwhelming. It can be something happening in the news, or an old argument with a friend, or whatever else makes you angry when you think about it.

How do you *know* you're angry? Anger, like every other emotion, is a physical experience in your body. Where do you feel sensations that you interpret as anger? Does your mouth get dry? Is your jaw tighter? Do you have to swallow? Are you getting a little bit of a headache? Are you dizzy? Do your shoulders tense up? Does your chest feel tight? Does your stomach hurt? Is your heart racing? These are just some of the common physical experiences that people get when they are angry. Most people find these physical sensations unpleasant and do something to try to avoid them. See how long you can just stay *with* the sensation and notice what happens as you do. Do you get more angry? Do other people or situations you are angry at come to mind? Do you feel yourself trying to flee from the feelings? Do you change position unintentionally to get away from the sensations? Do you start feeling confused? Is it hard to remember what you're angry about? Do you find that you're not feeling angry anymore and you don't know how and where the feeling went? Are you feeling depressed?

For many people it's hard to be angry because, like Heidi, they fear that their anger can destroy.

NOTE: If you have a history of violent behavior, don't do the next exercise. If you have hit your kids or your partner or anyone else in anger, you need to work differently than this and you should seek the help of a counselor.

EXERCISE

Take a few minutes to relax. Again, imagine any situation that *really* makes you angry. This time picture it as a video on a TV screen, so you're watching it instead of being in it. Give yourself complete permission to have any fantasy about your anger that presents itself. Try not to direct the fantasy consciously. Just let it play out on the screen. If you start to get anxious, or want to stop doing this exercise for any reason, first just imagine that you can press the "pause" button on the VCR. Now take a few minutes to look at the scene that made you want to stop watching. What is it about this scene that is unacceptable to you? Is your face contorted and ugly? Are you hitting someone? Are you being punished for being angry? Is someone hitting you? Are you about to be destroyed? Are you getting so stuck in the rage that it seems you'll never get out of it? Do you notice yourself fearing that this fantasy will come true? Just notice whatever your fantasy is about your anger. It's *just* a fantasy. It's only happening in your head and body. Just imagining it doesn't mean you will do it.

Let the VCR run some more and see where else your fantasy about anger takes you. Try this exercise every few days to help you get used to tolerating the feelings of anger in your body and to learn that thinking or imagining something doesn't make it happen in the real world. Chances are that the anger you saw in your fantasy was scary and out of control. In the fantasy you may have been screaming or hitting. This is actually rage. *Anger* can be experienced and expressed with a slightly raised voice, with only an angry expression, not a twisted, contorted face.

We have confused ideas about the difference between anger and rage for several reasons. If you are from a family where your parents yelled at each other a lot, then you may interpret yelling as being a necessary part of anger. If you come from a family where no anger of any kind was ever expressed, then *any* anger, no matter how appropriately expressed, may scare you. You may have learned about anger from TV. On TV people yell at each other a lot more than they do in real life and hit each other more often as well. If you learned about life from TV (and most of us have) then you are probably very confused about expressing anger. If anger is a problem you struggle with a lot in your life, talking to a counselor might help you be more appropriate in how you express your anger.

SELF PSYCHOLOGY THERAPY

Another psychodynamic therapy is called Self Psychology. Therapists who work from this perspective don't see depression as anger turned on the self. In this theory, depression is the result of not being able to soothe oneself after an emotional hurt. For many people, the ability to self-soothe is learned as an infant when parents provide care. We internalize this soothing comfort and then can draw on it whenever we need it. Sometimes the ability to draw on our skill of self-soothing is disrupted by an overwhelming crisis and we find ourselves flooded with anxiety, fear and sadness. Depression then numbs these unpleasant feelings but leaves us immobilized.

Sandy had had an abortion four years ago. Since then she had become increasingly depressed until she was unable to work. Sandy would have liked to continue the pregnancy. She was married and had two children. She enjoyed her pregnancies and loved being a mother but she and her husband Steve both had to work in order to support the family. Without her salary they would have had to get public assistance and this was unacceptable to both Sandy and Steve. They agreed she should have an abortion because they had no moral objection, and it was the wise thing to do in their situation.

Steve and Sandy were both prepared to feel sad after the abortion and they did. Steve was able to grieve and recover but Sandy felt nothing but deep sadness that wouldn't end. In a few months she was having a hard time concentrating and her motivation was gone. She kept going to work because she had to, but it was a struggle. She was too tired to pay much attention to her children or to Steve and their marriage went flat. Everyone was confused and miserable but no one in the family understood what was going on. Sandy had lost sight of the fact that her complete lack of interest in her life was the result of the feelings she had after the abortion.

Steve had a brief affair. He felt guilty and stupid for doing it but also recognized that he had been starving for any form of relationship and that this had made him look elsewhere for affection and attention. He was also angry at Sandy for being unavailable to him emotionally and sexually. He told Sandy about the affair and asked her forgiveness but also demanded that she or they go to counseling to try to figure out what was going wrong in their marriage.

When she came to see me, it was immediately apparent that Sandy was severely depressed. Her voice and facial expression were flat and she had little energy for answering my questions about her symptoms and how long they had lasted. Her memory was poor and she cried on and off throughout the interview. Steve had driven her to the appointment but she wanted to be seen alone because she didn't have the energy to have a discussion with him and me at the same time.

I explained the illness of depression to her and later to Steve, and suggested that I see her twice a week for a while. I also suggested seeing a psychiatrist for antidepressant medication but Sandy didn't want to take "drugs" for something she still believed was just laziness on her part.

At our next appointment I began taking a history and soon discovered that Sandy's depression followed her abortion. She wasn't sure there was any connection. As she told the story it became more clear that she had never grieved for the baby she would have liked to have had. She had just shut down completely into depression. The rest of her history helped explain why Sandy had become depressed.

Sandy grew up the youngest daughter in a family of four children where feelings were not allowed at all. The phrases she remembered hearing most often were, "Wipe that look off your face young lady," and "If you think you're sad now, I'll really give you something to be sad about." The implied threat of violence worked to keep order in the home because Sandy's oldest brother had challenged his father repeatedly and had been beaten up several times before he ran away from home. When children witness violence, it has a powerful impact on them. Even if they were not physically abused, the implied threat of being beaten is enough to make them fearful and passive.

Because it was never safe to show feelings it became unsafe to be aware of them. Sandy never had an opportunity to be comforted when she was sad or scared, to be admired when she was proud of herself for a good grade from school, or to have people join in her laughter when she found something funny. As a result, she never learned to comfort herself when she had painful feelings or to be proud of herself for her achievements.

Sandy and Steve married when they were nineteen and Steve provided much of the emotional support Sandy had missed during her childhood. The deep sadness Sandy felt after the abortion needed more soothing than one person could provide and Steve had been somewhat withdrawn at the time doing his own grieving. Sandy didn't have the skills to comfort herself. Her sadness was unbearable, and because she couldn't soothe herself when she was sad, she shut down into depression. In fact, Sandy *had* been depressed most of her life because it was the only coping mechanism that worked for her. It had been a mild depression and because it was all she had ever known, she assumed it was just how life was.

The work we did together took several years. Sandy needed to learn to feel her emotions and to soothe herself so she could experience her feelings without shutting down. After reading a number of books on depression and discussing medication with me for a long time, Sandy began taking Prozac and her depression lifted entirely. She still needed therapy to continue the work of identifying her feelings and learning to soothe the painful ones and enjoy the pleasant ones.

If you were neglected or abused as a child, you may not have the skill of self-soothing available to you, and you will be more prone to depression than someone who has been well nurtured. This doesn't mean that you can't learn to nurture and soothe yourself. Like Sandy, working with a therapist, you can gain this ability.

CONCLUSION

This chapter has covered a lot of territory. While there are a number of theories on depression and how to treat it, the most important thing to remember is that it is an illness of the body affecting the organ of brain, that leaves you thinking and feeling differently than you normally would. If you believe you are depressed, you should seek some kind of help immediately. Don't let society's confusion about "mental illness" stop you. If cognitive therapy works for you, do the exercises you need to every day. If you need talk therapy, find it. If your therapist suggests anti-depressant medication, seriously consider taking it. Become educated about depression by reading about it in some of the books on the reading list at the end of this book.

7

SPIRITUAL INJURY

This chapter is not about religion. It is about the spiritual conflict abortion can throw you into even if you hadn't thought of yourself as a spiritual person. My definition of spiritual injury comes from my clients. For them, it is the seemingly unfixable separation of themselves from what is "most essential" to their sense of self. This can be God, or it can be a less defined sense of their own goodness. For some women, this separation is felt as an inability to participate in the life of their church. Many Catholic women I have seen have felt unable to go to confession or receive communion after an abortion. Non-religious women suffering spiritual injury may feel they can't connect in a meaningful way with the most important people in their lives. They may feel cut off from their parents, partners, or children. At the moment they need Spirit most, they feel unable to touch it.

I wrote briefly in the chapter on how abortion distress manifests itself about a woman named Manuela. She had come to a workshop I presented to a group of social workers about *Peace After Abortion*. Like many of the participants, she was there partially to learn new skills and partially for her own self-healing. She was very brave. For the first time in her life she told the story of her abortion.

> She had become pregnant as a teenager. This alone was a source of shame to her, because she was a practicing Catholic and believed that premarital sex was a sin. She compounded her sin by having an illegal abortion. She did it because she had been certain that if her parents found out she was pregnant they would be terribly disappointed in her. When she married in her twenties, she was too ashamed of the sin the abortion represented to her to tell her husband about it. They tried for several years, but had difficulty conceiving a child. Manuela was convinced that she was being punished by God for having had the abortion. She felt harmful to her husband because her punishment was now hurting him as well, and she was lying to him by not telling him that it was all her fault. She eventually conceived and had a difficult pregnancy and dangerous childbirth in which she almost died. She took this hardship as proof that she had to pay dearly to make up for her sinfulness.

She had been burdened with her sense of sinfulness, of separation from God, for thirty years. She had felt that she deserved punishment, and that God, who could forgive anyone else, would never forgive her. Manuela's experience was a nightmare of believing she was cut off from God forever. She had never confessed to a priest because she was certain she would hear the words she already "knew" to be true: that she was damned to live separately from God and everyone she loved for eternity.

Spiritual injury is frequently surrounded by shame and guilt but it is not only about these emotions. Clients describe it as a sense of having lost their core self, or as having lost their anchor to the life around them. They feel disconnected and adrift.

June came to therapy because she felt confused, unfocused, and unproductive. She wasn't in crisis but she was concerned about herself. She was usually a dynamic, active woman with many interests and commitments, but now she didn't have the energy or the desire to get involved with the things that usually gave her pleasure. This certainly sounded like depression to me, and she did meet all the diagnostic criteria for depression. In telling me her history, June said her depression seemed to have started about two years before. As she said it she immediately made the connection to the abortion she had had around that time. This surprised her a lot because she had been very clear at the time that she didn't want to have children and that the abortion was a wise decision. She had raised her two bothers and sister after her mother died of cancer when June was eleven. Her father had retreated into his grief and then buried himself in his work. June was left alone to be the mom in her family.

June was committed to a woman's right to abortion and had worked on the political campaigns of pro-choice candidates. As we talked, June became more distressed and confused. She worried that her commitment to women's equality was somehow changing and that she was becoming an anti-choice radical. We investigated her beliefs and it was clear that she was the same person she had always been. So what was going on?

We spent the next session working on cognitive techniques to combat the symptoms of her depression. We talked a little about the benefits and drawbacks of medication, but it was still unclear why June had become depressed at all after the abortion.

June came to her next session and told me a dream she had had two nights before. She was sitting in a beautiful field surrounded by trees. There was a lake with birds on it and a gentle, warm breeze. June was sitting next to the lake nursing a baby! She was surprised even during her dream that she was enjoying this so much. The wind picked up and a huge wave came off the lake and engulfed her and the baby. When she got to the surface of the water, the baby was gone. June had woken up from this dream feeling more depressed than she had before.

As I questioned her about different parts of the dream it became clear that June wasn't feeling like she had been harmful to the baby. She couldn't have helped what had happened either in her dream or in her life. The pregnancy had resulted from a condom failure and she was still certain that she didn't ever want to have children.

Suddenly June stopped talking and seemed lost in thought. The baby in her dream wasn't the baby she had aborted, it was herself. She had lost an essential part of herself. As we explored what part of herself she felt she had lost, June dropped her head and began to cry. She said she had lost her sense of herself as warm, loving and nurturing. She had felt cold ever since the abortion. In fact she realized that she had been physically cold ever since then, needing to put on a sweater or take a hot shower to warm up more often than before the abortion. Being warm and nurturing was the center around which her self-concept was built. Now June understood; she was no longer able to believe in herself as loving—she wasn't able to connect with the part of herself that felt most like *her*.

As we worked together, other parts of June's spiritual injury came to light. The feeling of not being nurturing enough was painfully connected to not having been able to keep her mother alive, and then not being a good enough mother to her younger siblings. June knew intellectually, and in a very adult way, that she couldn't have saved her mother from dying. She began to understand that she had done the best she could with her sister and brothers—after all she was only a girl herself when she became responsible for their care.

I gently explained to June my understanding of spiritual injury. You *can't* be cut off from what is most essential to you. You don't stop being a good person, a warm and loving person, when you have an abortion, or when your mother dies, or when any other painful things happen in your life. The feeling that you are cut off from whatever is most essential to you is a delusion.

What creates the painful delusions we suffer with? In June's case it became apparent as we worked that she had created the delusion of separation from her warm heart as a self-punishment for her mother's death. This was complicated work because June is not a religious person and hadn't thought of herself as having a spiritual dimension and yet that is exactly where her pain was. Her spirit had been injured.

Manuela's spiritual injury was much more understandable to her. Her religion had clear rules which she had violated and she too punished herself for going against the rules by creating the delusion that she could be cut off forever from God.

The important point here is that you *can't* be separated from God, or your own goodness, or your place in the human family, or whatever else you understand is essential to your self. This is the heart of every spiritual tradition. Even though this teaching may be perverted and destroyed by many people who thump their chest and claim to be speaking for God, the core teaching of all the great religions is that we are inseparable from God, Creation, the Eternal, whatever creative force we feel is essential to our lives. The belief that you are separated from the Essential in your life is a belief *you have created* yourself to punish yourself in a terrible way.

Ironically, for Christian women, the "sin" is not the abortion, or a parent's death, or anything else; the sin of separating yourself from God and from God's forgiveness is much more serious than having the abortion. This refusal to be forgiven by God suggests that you are bigger than God in some way—more demanding, more sure about what is right and wrong.

In addition to the spiritual dimension of this injury, there is often just basic psychology fueling the sense of separation from the Essential. Little children think in a completely different way than adults do. Children believe that their thoughts are so powerful that just thinking something can make it happen. For example, when children are angry at their parents they often wish their parents would die. Because they believe in the power of their

Spiritual Injury 111

thoughts, they then get fearful that their parents *will* die. They become fearful and guilty and feel isolated from their parents. The belief that your thoughts have power over the external world is called "magical thinking." In any stressful situation we tend to regress—to return to a younger way of being, an earlier stage in our emotional development. Abortions are frequently stress-filled situations and so there is usually some regression.

Magical thinking seems to be a regressed part of spiritual injury. It may have seemed cruelly unfair to you that you became pregnant and had to make a decision about having an abortion. You may have felt angry at God for putting you in this painful situation. Then the "magic" in magical thinking begins: "If I'm mad at God, God must be mad at me too." Magical thinking explains the deluded belief that we can ever be separated from what is most essential to us.

Another aspect of regressing to an earlier emotional stage in our life when we are stressed, is feeling grandiose. Around age two, children develop a huge sense of power and self-importance. This is a normal part of human development, and if parents are admiring and impressed, the child will develop a healthy sense of self-esteem. If parents ignore or humiliate a child in this grandiose stage of development, the child will feel worthless and pathetic. If parents use their child's grandiosity to pump up their own flagging self-esteem, the child will grow up stuck in this grandiose, narcissistic stage. Sometimes the spiritual injury of abortion is a regression to the normal grandiosity of the two year old. Grandiosity can be positive, "I'm the smartest little girl anywhere in the world!" or it can be negative, "No one has ever been as bad as I have." It is this big badness that gets stirred up by abortion. If you believe that no one has ever been as bad as you, then how can God possibly ever forgive you, or how can you ever forgive yourself?

How do you heal from this spiritual injury? The first step is to get a clear understanding of the impulse to punish yourself. It may be only about the abortion. It may be clear to you now that your anxiety and denial about the pregnancy hid deeper beliefs about the sacredness of human life at every stage of development. Or, like June, the abortion may represent something else in your life that has unconsciously felt like a failing that you need to be punished for.

The second step is to talk to someone about your abortion. If you are a member of a church, temple, mosque or religious group of any kind, consider talking to someone from your spiritual family about the abortion and your feelings of spiritual injury. It doesn't have to be the minister, priest, rabbi, or nun. It should be whomever you admire and trust most in the congregation. Choose the person you have found to be most loving, fair and forgiving. Keep in mind that your minister has probably heard everything there is to know about human nature from the other members of your church, and may be far more understanding than you can imagine. Read Chapter Nine, *Talking About It*, for ideas and suggestions on how to talk to someone from your spiritual community about your abortion. If you are not a member of a religious body, find a good friend or a good psychotherapist to help you sort through your spiritual injury. There is information on how to find a therapist in Chapter Nine.

You can work on healing spiritual injury yourself. The heart of healing from spiritual injury related to abortion is self-forgiveness. I have mentioned self-forgiveness in the chapters on guilt and shame, and forgiving others in the chapter on depression and anger. I return to forgiveness so much because it is the best medicine there is for the kinds of pain stirred up by an abortion and because forgiveness is a skill we don't learn very well in our culture. Chapter Ten, *Self-forgiveness, Atonement, and Ritual*, can help you start learning the art of self-forgiveness.

    The third step in healing spiritual injury is to practice what you have learned from whomever you have talked to and from the chapter on *Self-forgiveness, Atonement, and Ritual*. Practice means that forgiveness is not a one-time event. Forgiveness takes time, patience, insight, and the ability to learn to really treat yourself lovingly.

8

SOMETIMES MEN HAVE TROUBLE WITH ABORTION TOO

This chapter is for men. It may be that your partner's abortion has caused you emotional or spiritual distress. Reading the rest of this book will help you understand what your girlfriend or wife may be experiencing, and can help you heal from your own post-abortion pain.

(If you are the partner of a man having difficulty after your abortion you should read this chapter too because it may help give you insight into what he may be feeling.)

For many men, the hardest thing about a partner's abortion is that it is completely out of their control. Men in our culture are raised to be comfortable when they are in control of their environment. When they find themselves with no power or control, they may get anxious and angry. A woman's pregnancy is truly out of your control. The last moment you have any control in pregnancy is when you put on a condom prior to intercourse, or don't put one on. This may seem cold or blunt but it is just the way things are. The reality that your moment of control has passed can lead to a lot of painful feelings. Some men feel angry about not having a legal say in the outcome of the pregnancy. Some feel guilty for not trying to prevent the pregnancy, or for trying but being unsuccessful. They see everything that happens after not using a condom, or the condom breaking, as completely their fault. Some feel guilty for the physical or emotional pain their partners struggle with during or after the abortion. Some men feel shame for *not* feeling as bad as their partner about the abortion. Some men are confused when their partners are OK with having had an abortion, but they themselves are depressed, guilty, grieving, or shame-filled.

As you read through this chapter, look at how depression, guilt, grief and shame are defined in chapters three through six. If one of these feelings seems to be what is troubling you, also read the chapter on that specific feeling. Adapt the exercises in that chapter and do them as many times as you need to. Then read Chapter Ten, *Self-forgiveness, Atonement, and Ritual.*

DEPRESSION

Andy had been depressed ever since his girlfriend Nicole's abortion five months before. Nicole had finally realized that his mood change had come at the same time as her pregnancy, and had called Planned Parenthood for a referral to a therapist. After I had talked to them together in the first session, Andy said he would like to see me alone. I am not a couple's counselor so I was relieved, and it was clear that Andy was the person in pain, so this arrangement felt like it would work out. If Andy and Nicole ended up needing ongoing couple's counseling, I would have referred them to several other excellent therapists.

Andy wanted to see me alone because he was feeling hurt by Nicole but didn't understand why and didn't want to start working it out with her until he understood it himself. He said he was having trouble sleeping, couldn't understand what he was reading for school and had started doing poorly on tests. Much of the time he was fatigued and felt hopeless about most things in his life. He told me about the month leading up to the abortion. He knew intellectually that this was not the time for them to have a baby. They were in their mid-twenties and still in school. Having a child would force one of them, probably Nicole, to put her career on hold. Andy felt strongly that it would have been unfair to ask Nicole to do this and he never talked with her about it. She had been very clear from the beginning that she wanted to have an abortion and Andy had respected her decision.

As we talked for the next few weeks, emotions Andy had been unaware of began to surface. He had felt isolated and lonely after Nicole had a positive pregnancy test. He realized that he had wanted her to see and sense his ambivalence about the abortion. He was astounded to discover this ambivalence himself. He hadn't let himself feel the yearning he had to be a father; to bring his baby to Nicole at night for a feeding, or to take him with him when he went to the market or to school. These were deeply painful realizations and Andy was embarrassed by the tears he shed as he talked about these newly discovered wishes. He grieved the little boy he felt he had let down so completely but grieving alone didn't help his depression.

We returned to the feelings of loneliness Andy had felt when Nicole had not understood intuitively what he really wanted from the pregnancy. Had he ever felt like this before? It was hard for him to remember. After a few more sessions Andy came in one day feeling very sad, but proud of himself for gaining insight between sessions into what his depression was about. He *had* felt this way before! When he was seven, his parents had divorced after a difficult marriage. Andy remembered that much of his childhood was spent listening to his parents fight late at night. They could never seem to agree on anything. When they finally divorced, Andy was confused and scared. His father left the state and only saw Andy and his sister for a few weeks in the summer and at Christmas. Andy's mother was fearful and distracted. She worked long hours to support her kids and her mother who lived with them.

There were several ways in which Andy's childhood, and his experience of the abortion, felt similar. He now understood that he hadn't realized how much he wanted to continue the pregnancy because disagreeing with Nicole felt too similar to listening to his parents fight. He unconsciously defended himself against those unhappy memories by not getting into a fight with Nicole.

Nicole's inability to read Andy's deepest thoughts was what had caused the depression. He knew that she couldn't read his mind. He even knew that it wasn't her job to try to read his mind, but it felt just like his mother's distraction and unavailability after the divorce. Andy realized that he had become depressed then, and that the same sense of isolation, of not being understood, had led to his current depression.

Andy brought Nicole to his last two sessions. With my support, he told her about his feelings during and after her pregnancy and how they related to his childhood. She was able to hear this without feeling attacked or blamed. With her empathy and understanding, Andy felt less lonely and less depressed. Being able to talk openly about their feelings about the abortion allowed them to talk more honestly about other aspects of their relationship and they left therapy feeling much closer and more able to care for each other.

Depression is an illness that changes the chemistry of the brain. For many people, stressful events in life lead to temporary changes in brain chemistry but then the brain returns to normal. Sometimes, the body can't return brain chemistry to normal and like Andy, a long-standing depression sets in. Therapy and medication can both help heal long-term depression. If like Andy, you are sleeping too little, or too much; if you have difficulty concentrating, are eating more or less than usual, feel hopeless, helpless, tearful or suicidal, please read Chapter Six of this book, *Depression and Anger*, and if you recognize that you are depressed, seek help immediately.

GUILT

There are many things you may feel guilty about after your partner's abortion. Not using condoms; not thinking carefully about how your partner would feel about an unplanned pregnancy or after an abortion; not feeling able to do the honorable, "manly" thing and help her raise your child; forcing the issue of abortion by threatening to leave your partner if she refused to have an abortion. Or, you may have acted completely responsibly in all ways and *still* feel guilty. Guilt is the painful sense of having harmed someone through your own action or inaction.

Bud was a huge, scary-looking Hell's Angel covered in tattoos. He had come to therapy with his girlfriend of three years, Cindi, because they were both feeling terrible since her abortion. She had wanted to continue the pregnancy. She was Catholic and believed that abortion was taking a human life and was a mortal sin. Bud had insisted, using various means of coercion including threatening to leave and beating Cindi once while they were arguing about the pregnancy. She had the abortion. Then she felt the most straight-forward guilt about harming the baby I had ever seen, and she was angry at Bud for forcing her to have the abortion.

Bud's guilt was much more complicated. He was responding to how bad Cindi was feeling and realizing that it was he who had hurt her so deeply by insisting that she have the abortion. He started to have nightmares. He was wading chest-high through a swamp filled with the arms, legs, torsos and heads of tiny babies. He would wake up in a panic from these horrifying dreams and be too afraid to go back to sleep. As he became more exhausted he became more panic-filled until he felt certain that he was going to have a psychotic break.

I asked him what the dreams were like. It was difficult for him to answer at first. He finally said they were like the dreams he had had in Viet Nam and for the year after returning from the war while he was psychiatrically hospitalized. He had been on anti-psychotic medication for several years after that and had learned ways to cope with his severe Post-traumatic Stress Disorder (PTSD).

PTSD is a disorder with specific symptoms that can follow any psychologically distressing event that is outside the range of usual experience. This can be a natural disaster, war, being the victim of a violent crime like rape, or seeing someone else suffer serious injury or death in an accident or crime. The symptoms of PTSD include remembering the traumatic event over and over again, having recurring nightmares about the event, psychological distress when you see, hear, or smell something that reminds you of the trauma, and occasionally, reliving the event as though you were going through it again. People with PTSD consciously avoid anything that will remind them of the trauma and can become emotionally numb and feel disconnected from the life around them. They also have symptoms of central nervous system agitation like difficulty falling or staying asleep, angry outbursts, difficulty concentrating and an exaggerated startle response.

Bud saw how the abortion was like his terrible experiences in Viet Nam. He had felt that his own survival was in jeopardy and he had used force and violence in both situations to protect himself. In Viet Nam he had killed many people. He had survived while his friends had died.

Cindi's pregnancy had felt dangerous to him. His world felt threatened and he had reacted as though he were still in Viet Nam, with coercion and force. Until the abortion was over, he couldn't take Cindi's feelings into account, he was just trying to survive. After the abortion he realized how much he had hurt her and he was overwhelmed with guilt. He felt guilty for sacrificing Cindi and the baby so he could survive. His current guilt was fueled by his unhealed guilt about killing soldiers and civilians in Viet Nam and about having survived while his friends died. Once Bud understood how the abortion had reactivated his PTSD we could work on self-forgiveness and he could use the coping skills he had created to soothe himself in stressful times.

Bud's guilt was based on out-of-the-ordinary life experience. Most men's guilt after an abortion is not as dramatically clear cut. Most often, when men feel guilty after an abortion it is about not having been able to fulfill their obligations and really take care of their partner or baby. This sounds old-fashioned but our culture still sees this kind of responsibility as the man's job and we still socialize boys more than girls to accept this as their role. Overcoming guilt about not fulfilling role obligations doesn't mean you have to stop caring for the people you love. It is important to recognize though that men are under extraordinary pressure to carry the load for their families. Even though most women now work, most men and women still cling to the wish that the man provide for his family, so the woman doesn't really have to work. Just notice how you feel when you think about your wife or girlfriend making double the amount of money you do. Uncomfortable? Then you are caught, along with most other people, in the prison of unreasonable expectations about men's obligations to provide for everyone around them. You don't have to be better than your neighbor, or your wife or girlfriend, at taking care of your family, you only have to do your best and then have a sense of humor about the unreasonable demands that society will still place on you. Getting to this point will require self-forgiveness, and reading Chapter Ten, *Self-forgiveness, Atonement, and Ritual*, will help.

GRIEF

Jose called to make an appointment for himself and his wife before she had her abortion. She was frantic to have the abortion but he wanted to talk to someone to make sure it was the right decision. He really wanted to talk her out of it because he couldn't understand why she was so adamant about terminating the pregnancy.

Nola and Jose came together to the appointment and gave me a little of their history. They were both educators and had two daughters, seven and nine years old. They were both totally committed to being parents and honored and acknowledged each other for their commitment to their children. This is what was so confusing to Jose. He knew what a great mom Nola was and he knew that he really had always done as much of the parenting in the family as she had. He knew they could raise another child. Nola cried quietly as Jose explained his confusion to me. He excused himself so she could talk to me alone because it was obvious that she had something troubling her that she couldn't share with him.

Nola shared with me that she had become panic stricken when she had the first symptoms of pregnancy. She was having trouble sleeping and couldn't eat, she was exhausted all the time and she just wanted the pregnancy over right now! She felt irresponsible for having this feeling but she was certain that she couldn't continue the pregnancy.

Her history explained why. Nola's father had been abusive and neglectful. Her mother had five children and, it seemed to Nola, was always pregnant or completely exhausted. When she was fifteen, her father refused to support her any more and she had to work after school to have money for clothes, food, and the other necessities of life except rent. She put herself through college and then got married. Jose was the opposite of her father. He was loving, gentle, caring and attentive to her. They had similar spiritual backgrounds and beliefs, and agreed on the important things in family life—how to manage money and how to raise kids. They worked for several years to save enough money so that Nola could take several years off from teaching to have babies. And then they had their two daughters and raised them together.

Nola's panic was about needing time for herself. The thought of having another totally dependent baby in the house felt too much like a repeat of her mother's life. The problem was that she knew intellectually that Jose was going to be there 100% and that he would love to raise another child and she felt awful for hurting him.

Jose returned to the session and Nola and I explained the source and depth of her need to have an abortion. He understood, but he was very sad. He didn't want to show his sadness because he didn't want to hurt Nola. I encouraged him to tell her about his sadness and let her see it so they could each be honest with the other and get some of what they needed from each other.

Jose cried a little. He wanted this baby because he loved children. He had devoted his life to kids as an educator and to his own kids and even though this was an unplanned pregnancy, he was already devoted to this child. He also recognized that Nola had to want it too, and that if she didn't then they shouldn't have it, but he was still sad and grieving for this child.

I saw Jose alone for one more session just to help him grieve. Nola had had the abortion in the meantime, and Jose had gone with her to provide support. It had been very hard on him because the clinic they went to didn't allow partners to stay with the women during the abortion. He had had to sit in the waiting room for several hours and just wonder what was happening to Nola and to the baby he wanted so badly to have. Jose had a lot of fantasies while he was waiting; he would barge through the door and stop the procedure; Nola would come out smiling and tell him that she had changed her mind and that they would have this baby after all; an anti-choice crazy would call in a bomb scare and put the procedure off and Nola would change her mind; or the crazy would throw the bomb and they would all be killed; the doctor would make a terrible mistake and Nola would die on the table and he'd be left to raise their children alone. He got more and more anxious as he waited. When Nola came out of recovery she was tired but relieved and even happy to have this ordeal behind her.

Jose was sad as we talked. It had been over two weeks since the abortion but he couldn't shake the sadness he felt. It was there from the time he woke up until the time he fell asleep and even crept into his dreams. He felt he was over-reacting. After all, he had never known this baby really, never held it or changed its diaper or sang to it. He knew rationally that it hadn't been a baby at all but an early embryo too tiny to see with the naked eye—so why was he so sad? We explored what Jose knew about the process of grief. He believed that it shouldn't last too long and that really it didn't make sense to grieve this much over a being who had never existed and whom he had never met. Not seeing the baby seemed to be a theme.

I suggested Jose create a collage of his experience so he would have something tangible to look at to help him grieve. At first he felt that this was silly, but he could quickly recognize that it was actually scary to him. He felt that if he created an image of the baby and said good-bye to it, the sadness he was holding in check would be hard to bear. Jose was brave and willing to try, and the exercise stirred up more grief, loss, and sadness than he had felt up to this point. He was surprised to find that he could stop crying after a few minutes and felt more at ease with the loss of the baby.

Jose called back two weeks later to say that he was feeling much better. He had cried a few times more and now was only having twinges of grief when he saw little babies. I reminded him that the date on which Nola would have had the baby if she had continued the pregnancy, and the anniversary of the abortion next year, might also stir up some unfinished grief.

If you feel that you are grieving, read the whole chapter on grief in this book and do the exercises in a way that makes sense to you.

SHAME

Shame feelings come out of a sense of being flawed, a lousy person, not worthwhile. Shame feelings are about embarrassment, humiliation, and feeling exposed for the basically rotten person you feel you are but that you try to keep secret from the rest of the world. Sometimes men feel shame rather than guilt about not being able to provide for their partners during pregnancy. They suffer with the gnawing feeling that if only they weren't so incompetent, unmotivated, young, unfocused... they would have been able to help their partner have a baby. Other men's shame comes from the fear of exposure of their irresponsible behavior.

> Carl was a man in his forties who came to me because he was enraged with his girlfriend for becoming pregnant and having an abortion. For a few weeks it was hard to understand exactly what the problem was because Carl's rage was making his thinking and behavior erratic and hard to follow. He couldn't tell me what part of the abortion was so infuriating. After a few weeks of coming twice a week and sometimes pacing around my office yelling in anger, Carl could settle down and organize his thinking better. We soon discovered that under the rage was a terrible sense of shame about almost every aspect of Carl's behavior during this episode. It was difficult to stay with the shameful feelings, and Carl would almost immediately fly into a rage again as a way to avoid the pain of shame. Over time we could stay with and explore the shame for longer periods of time and understand where they had come from.

Carl didn't like using condoms and would sometimes cajole his girlfriend Mandy into unprotected intercourse. They weren't worried about HIV because they had both been tested and trusted each others' commitment to the relationship. They used condoms as their method of birth control because Mandy couldn't use hormone birth control for medical reasons and she'd had difficulty with the diaphragm in the past and didn't trust it.

Eventually, Mandy had become pregnant and was ambivalent about having a baby. She said if Carl wanted to continue the pregnancy that she would like to, but she wasn't willing to do it without his complete support. Carl was ambivalent too. He had a twenty-year-old son from a previous marriage whom he had not been involved with for over ten years. He knew he liked young kids and being a dad, but was worried about being an "old" dad and about the financial responsibility. In the end he told Mandy he couldn't promise he would be able to stay with her if she had the baby. Mandy had the abortion and then was angry with Carl for getting her pregnant in the first place.

Shame was almost impossible for Carl to tolerate. He would drop his head and bury his face in his hands. As we talked about shame, Carl noticed that his chest tightened and he felt short of breath, his face flushed and his stomach knotted. He would remember over and over again each thing he had done that he was ashamed of: seducing Mandy out of using a condom, being fearful of taking on new financial responsibilities, not offering unconditional support to Mandy whatever decision she made, and ultimately hurting Mandy by his own indecisiveness. Carl felt each of these acts was evidence of his pathetically flawed nature. The pregnancy just brought to light feelings of worthlessness Carl usually kept buried out of conscious awareness.

I asked him about the earliest times he could remember feeling flawed and worthless. It seemed to him that he had always felt this way. He remembered feeling awkward at school because he had been taller than other kids, and by junior high, bigger than his teachers as well. He had been clumsy because his body was always growing and his coordination was a few years behind. Because he was big, people thought he was older than he was and expected him to be able to do things he wasn't capable of. His parents had the same unreasonable expectations and frequently yelled at him for being inept and childish. Over the weeks it became clear that Carl's parents were in fact quite verbally and emotionally abusive. He had never thought of them as abusing him because like most people, he equated abuse with being beaten up or molested.

At first, he dismissed the idea of emotional abuse as just an excuse for being a lousy person. As we explored this more it became clear that "making excuses" for why he couldn't be as mature as his parents expected him to be was another piece of the emotional abuse. He had never been listened to when he tried to explain himself; he had been told to "stop making excuses and whining." So if he recognized and talked about the abuse, the old abusive messages he had gotten as a child would arise to abuse him more and he would feel that he was a pathetic whiner. It felt like an unending, circular trap.

We went over the events of the pregnancy to see how they fit in with the abusive messages Carl had gotten as a child. Not using a condom was "immature," something he was forever being accused of. Not wanting to take on further financial responsibilities was also evidence of immaturity, as well as irresponsibility and weakness, two accusations his dad in particular made about him throughout his teens. And hurting Mandy started a rerun of abuse he had received from his mother about how his ineptness and stupidity were a pain to her all the time.

In fact, Carl was still taking care of his mother by sending her money every month even though she had a fine retirement income. Carl realized that sending his mom money now was an unconscious way to atone for what a bad kid he had always believed himself to be. The irony was that he felt shame for hurting Mandy because he couldn't promise to support her, because he was trying to support his mother to redeem himself from shame.

Carl's work focused on healing the wounds of the emotional abuse he had received as a child. The work included taking responsibility for the actions he was not proud of and making amends to Mandy. He also disengaged from his mother and stopped sending her money she didn't really need so he could support another child if he and Mandy decided to have one in the future. He called his son and re-established their relationship. With each act, he could experience himself as competent and mature.

Healing from shame is hard work and requires a great deal of self-forgiveness. Read the chapters in this book on *Shame, Talking About It*, and *Self-forgiveness, Atonement, and Ritual*.

Some men find that their partner's abortion has stirred up other kinds of old injuries and the unfinished feelings that go with them. One client was feeling caught in the swirl of never-dealt-with feelings about being adopted. Another had never been helped to grieve the drowning death of his little sister, and his partner's abortion opened the long-repressed grief he had been carrying around for twenty years.

Men, like women, don't always know what they are feeling or why they are acting the way they are. Some men find that they are acting in ways that are self-destructive and counterproductive after a partner's abortion. They will find themselves compelled to test fate by having unprotected intercourse and being involved in several more abortions. Or they will have trouble being sexual at all and may become impotent. Either of these scenarios will lead to more guilt, anger, shame, and grief, and all are destructive to any relationship you are in. If you recognize that you are acting differently since the abortion, read the chapter on *Talking About It*, and get yourself the help you need to sort out your feelings so you can return to a smart and healthy life.

Men don't get much recognition in our culture for having feelings. Until reading this chapter, you may have felt isolated and weird for having strong feelings about an abortion. You are not weird at all, but it may be hard to break down the feelings of isolation. The unfortunate stigma that still surrounds abortion makes it hard to talk to other men about your experience and discover that some of them also have strong feelings about a partner's abortion. Talking about it is exactly what you need to do. If it doesn't feel safe to talk to your friends about this, give yourself the gift of a few sessions with a therapist who can listen and help you sort out your feelings. It's tough work sometimes but it can help you feel like the man you want to be.

9

TALKING ABOUT IT

Talking about your abortion with someone else may sound dangerous and frightening to you. Fears about being judged as a bad person may overwhelm you. And yet talking about the abortion to someone safe can be profoundly healing. Once your abortion is no longer a secret, you may experience a sense of relief and liberation. In telling someone else about your abortion, you may find that you come to understand how or why you got pregnant in the first place. You may also remember aspects of the situation you had forgotten, and some of these may help you be forgiving toward yourself in a way you haven't been able to up to now.

How does keeping a secret hurt us? When we keep a secret, the only person we are listening to about the secret is ourselves. There is no other input, no other view or perspective to challenge our understanding of the situation. If you are depressed, then only the self-critical voice of your depression is being heard. There is no way to break out of the cycle of self-abusive language. If you are torturing yourself with guilt or shame, there is no one to suggest or offer forgiveness.

Keeping a secret is a stress-filled experience. You *always* have to be careful of what you say to others. You *always* have to be aware of where a conversation is going and try to steer it away from your secret. When something happens (like an anti-choice ad on TV) that stirs up your feelings about the abortion, you have to pretend you are OK even if you're not. The emotional stress from this can lead to serious physical problems. You may sleep poorly, find yourself "overemotional," angry for no reason, and depressed or anxious. You may develop full-blown panic attacks from keeping a secret.

Another way you can be hurt by keeping a secret is the damage it does to your self-esteem. Holding onto the secret may make you feel dishonest. It's like carrying around a container of poison inside yourself. As you hold more tightly to the secret, it squeezes out and contaminates your sense of being a good person. Now you are someone who has had an abortion *and* you are a liar. You may start to judge other things about yourself more harshly in light of this view of yourself as dishonest. You may feel that the dishonesty makes you unworthy of being loved by your partner, or makes you a bad parent to your children. You may decide you have to break up with your boyfriend or husband, or you may become distant from your children as a way not to contaminate them with your sense of badness.

Keeping a secret is ultimately about feeling cut off from the people who are most important to you. The longer the secret goes on, the more alone you feel. You may also experience this as being cut off from God, spirit, nature, whatever is most essential to your life. Secrets hurt us because they separate us from our own nature and humanity and we end up isolated and alone.

How does telling a secret heal? First, you put something that has only been inside you, out into the world. That simple act may be all you need. It may not matter as much as you thought it would how the person you've told reacts. Just the act of letting go of the secret will probably provide relief from the stress of keeping it.

If you have told someone who cares for you and wants to understand you, healing will come from getting their perspective. Now there is another point of view to look at your actions from. You get a different, and probably more forgiving opinion about your abortion. Having a perspective other than your own helps to break you out of the dark cycle of self-abusive thoughts. Now you are being challenged and reminded to look at aspects of your decision that you may have forgotten about in the process of keeping your secret.

Telling immediately breaks down the wall of isolation that the secret built between you and the people around you. You can begin to feel connected again to the people and things that are important to you. This return to connection *is* the healing that comes from telling your secret.

WHO IS SAFE TO TELL?

One reason for keeping the secret of your abortion is the belief that if others found out, they would judge you harshly or be disappointed in you. In deciding who to tell about your abortion, you need to pick someone who will not be judgmental or hurtful to you. This may seem like the easy way out. You may feel that the only "correct" person to tell is the one who will be the *most* angry, or disappointed, or hurt by what you have to say. Even if there is someone whom you feel you need to tell and who you are certain will be critical, it is wise to first tell someone who will be compassionate to you.

Think about all your friends, your family members, teachers, your pastor, parents of friends, anyone who comes to mind. Ask yourself five questions: 1) Have I ever heard this person's opinion on abortion in general? 2) Is their opinion dogmatic? (Have they used words like "all," "never," "should/shouldn't?" Or, did their opinion seem to take into account the circumstances of the individual woman they were talking about?) 3) Is this someone I have heard gossip about others? 4) Is this someone I have entrusted a secret to in the past and who has betrayed my trust? 5) Is this someone I want to feel closer to?

First, you want to make sure you are telling someone who does not have a strong and harsh opinion against abortion. (This may seem to rule out ever confessing the abortion if you're Catholic, but I'll get to that later in this chapter.) You may know someone who is uncomfortable about abortion but who is fair and non-judgmental. The fairness is far more important than the person's own beliefs about abortion.

Second, you want to make sure that the person you pick to tell your secret to is someone who can keep secrets. If you have a friend whom you gossip with about others, she or he may not be the best person to tell. This may sound unfair since you may have indulged in the gossip as much as the other person. This isn't about judging them or yourself for gossiping though, it's just about recognizing that they may not be the safest person to share a secret with because they're in the habit of telling secrets. You want to know too, that you are telling someone who has never betrayed your trust in the past.

When you have identified someone whom you find fair and non-judgmental, who doesn't gossip much and who has never betrayed your trust in the past, you need to think about how telling them will affect your relationship. Telling a secret may bring you much closer to this person. They could turn around and tell you a secret of their own. Perhaps she had an abortion too, or he got someone pregnant once. You need to decide if this is someone you might want to become closer to. Or, if they are not as trustworthy as you had thought, you may feel hurt by this person and your relationship could end. Is telling your secret to this particular person worth the risk?

Once you have picked someone to tell, make a plan about how to do it. Start by writing out what you want to say. Then practice the conversation in your head so that when you do tell them, it feels familiar. Ask the person to give you some time in a private place and tell them you need their help with something personal. Let them know *first* that what you want to talk to them about needs to be held in confidence and ask if they will promise you that.

Try to tell your story from the beginning. Tell about finding out you were pregnant and how that felt to you. Tell about the process you went through to make your decision to have the abortion. Tell about your feelings, as well as about the facts. When you are done, notice how you are feeling and share that with them, too. Also let them know what you worry they may be thinking or feeling about you now that they've heard your story.

There's no way to predict how telling your secret will be received. Hopefully, you will feel understood and cared for. You will probably feel more connected to yourself again and to the world around you. On the other hand, if the other person couldn't provide what you needed in a listener, you may be feeling foolish, humiliated, judged and betrayed. Don't let this stop you from trying to tell someone else who can be supportive.

HOW TO FIND A THERAPIST

If you couldn't think of anyone who felt trustworthy to you, or if you did but they let you down, don't give up. If there is no one safe to talk to in your life, then find a therapist. Therapists are trained to listen, and have worked with many other people who have struggled with issues of grief, depression, guilt, shame and low self-esteem. Sometimes it's hard to go to a professional for help because a therapist or counselor may seem like a poor substitute for a friend. You might even feel a little humiliated for having to pay someone to listen to your problems, but talking to a therapist can often help you more than talking to someone you know. Pastoral counselors can be helpful too, especially if you are struggling with a sense of spiritual injury.

There are important things to keep in mind when looking for a therapist or counselor. First, you want to find someone who can be compassionate and empathic. You should have a sense that this person cares about you and is really trying to understand you from your point of view. You can begin to get this sense from talking to the therapist on the phone when you call for an appointment. Expect a good therapist to be able to convey care and empathy in that first contact. The therapist should ask you questions to help determine what you need, what times you are available for an appointment, and should tell you the cost of therapy without making you ask.

Next, you want to know that this therapist meets the ethical standards for her or his profession. Each kind of therapist—Licensed Clinical Social Worker (LCSW), Marriage, Family and Child Counselor (MFCC), Psychologist (Ph.D.), or Psychiatrist (MD)—has a state agency that licenses them. You can call the agency and make sure there are no complaints lodged by clients against the therapist. Many therapists also belong to a professional organization (National Association of Social Workers, or American Psychological Association, for example) and at the state level, these organizations enforce ethical standards and can tell you if they have taken action against a therapist for ethics violations.

This may sound like therapists are dangerous people, but checking the ethics of important health care providers is always a good idea; you can and should investigate a physician or dentist you intend to go to in the same way. If *any* health care professional ever makes you feel uncomfortable or confused in any way, you should point this out to them and if their response does not make you more comfortable, you should consider terminating the relationship. If a therapist is telling you more than you want to know about themselves, tell them so, and if they continue to do this, stop seeing them. If a therapist *ever* suggests any kind of sexual contact or relationship between you, stop seeing him or her immediately and make a complaint to the appropriate licensing agency. Most therapists are competent and ethical. The few incompetent or unethical ones can cause you serious harm and you need to protect yourself from them.

One way to make sure you are going to see a good therapist is to get a referral from someone you know and trust. If you are uncomfortable asking around for a good therapist, then call an agency like Planned Parenthood or other family planning clinic in your area and see if they keep a list of therapists they trust. Ask how they screen therapists on their referral list. You can also ask your doctor for referrals.

You may be seeking a spiritually based counselor rather than a professional therapist. If so, keep the same ideas in mind about compassion, empathy and ethics. Don't assume, if you are Catholic or from a fundamentalist church, that your priest or pastor will be judgmental of you. Look back at the list of five questions to ask yourself when you are trying to decide whom to tell. Does your pastor or priest preach about compassion for women who have abortions? He may indeed be safe to talk to.

If you are Catholic, call Catholic Charities in your area and ask if they have a Project Rachel group. This is a post-abortion group for Catholic women and it should be supportive and encouraging rather than condemning. If your priest or pastor doesn't seem like a safe person to talk to, visit other churches for a few weeks and see if you can find a pastor who seems more compassionate on this issue than your own. As long as you find a pastor who is compassionate, his views on abortion actually may not be an issue. You can also call *Catholics for a Free Choice* for more information.

Many Protestant denominations and ministers support abortion rights. Some Planned Parenthood affiliates know these people and can refer you to them.

Telling the secret of your abortion is not going to be easy. Even if the abortion is not a secret, many of your feelings about it may be. Talking about them to someone who can listen without judgment may be painful, but will be a major step in healing from your post-abortion distress.

10

SELF-FORGIVENESS, ATONEMENT, AND RITUAL

FORGIVENESS

In reading through the chapters of this book you may have discovered feelings of having harmed yourself or someone else in some way. You may have identified shame as the feeling that is causing you pain. You may still be angry at your partner, friends, or parents for pressuring you to have an abortion, or abandoning you when you felt most in need. Guilt, shame, and anger may seem untreatable and unforgivable, but they are not. The treatment for shame and guilt is self-forgiveness. The treatment for anger is forgiveness. Forgiveness and self-forgiveness are often the most important skills you can learn for healing the post-abortion distress you are struggling with.

WHAT FORGIVENESS IS NOT

Forgiveness (including self-forgiveness) is not the same thing as forgetting. Very often we hear the phrase "forgive and forget," and we believe that to do one is to do the other. You may worry that if you forget your mistakes, or injuries to yourself or others, that you will repeat them, so forgiving seems like a foolish and self-destructive thing to do. You may worry that if you forgive others, you will forget to protect yourself from the person who harmed you and you will be hurt again. Because of this confusion, you may be living in painful guilt, shame or anger much of the time; unable to let go of these feelings because you are afraid to forget.

See if you can remember a time in the distant past when someone hurt your feelings. Try to find an incident that doesn't stir up any anger or humiliation when you call it to mind. Where did those feelings go? Perhaps, without knowing it, you have forgiven that person for hurting you. You have not forgotten the event—it just doesn't have the emotional punch it used to. When you forgive, you do not forget the events, you only liberate yourself from the painful feelings that used to haunt you.

Forgiveness is not condoning. When you actively forgive yourself or others you are not saying, "What I (or you) did is OK." You are just accepting the human frailties that can lead to hurtful behavior. You may not want to accept your own or others' frailties. One of the myths we learn about forgiveness is that if we accept our weaknesses and frailties, we will not be motivated to do anything to change them. The opposite is true. You cannot begin to heal or change yourself until you first accept who you are, and what you are, right now. As long as you hate the part of yourself that has acted hurtfully, you will spend a lot of energy trying to push it away rather than healing it, and you are more likely to repeat behaviors that you regret.

Forgiveness is not a sign of timidity, cowardice or weakness. This is in direct contradiction to many of our cherished cultural beliefs; the heroes in our most popular movies don't forgive their enemies—they blow them to pieces with assault weapons. The spouses of people who cheat on them are seen as weak and even stupid if they forgive their wife or husband and continue in the marriage. Inner city gangs and countries at war can't offer peace to each other because it will be believed that they are weak and about to lose anyway.

WHAT FORGIVENESS IS

Forgiveness is a process of strength and bravery. Paradoxically, it takes strength to accept your own weakness and frailty. It involves risk to share your most painful feelings with others as you work to forgive yourself. It feels risky to forgive someone else because there is no guarantee that they will respond to you in a positive way.

Forgiveness is the process of opening yourself to reconnection with whatever is most essential to you. It can be your relationship with yourself, with God, nature or the people you care about most. In forgiving yourself, and accepting how you are right now, you pave the way for moving in the direction you want to; for becoming more the person you want to be. In forgiving others, you remove the barriers you have put between you and them. *You* are more open to reconnection whether they are or not.

Forgiveness is a process of optimism. In working to forgive yourself, you are acknowledging that you are truly capable of change. In forgiving others, you are sending the message that you truly believe they can change.

Most specifically, forgiveness is the process of letting go. When you are unforgiving to yourself, you are holding tightly to anger at yourself, or shame, or guilt. To forgive means to let go of that anger, shame or guilt. Holding tightly to these painful feelings uses a lot of emotional energy and keeps you stuck right where you are. The only way to have more energy for changing into who you want to be, and more energy for moving forward with your life, is to let go of the painful feelings through self-forgiveness. Forgiving others also releases your energy for other things. The rest of this section will focus specifically on self-forgiveness, because many women working through post-abortion distress need a lot of work on forgiving themselves first.

The most important word in the above paragraphs is *process*. Self-forgiveness is not a one-time act. It is a repeated process of consciously working to forgive yourself. The process involves giving yourself a little time each day to focus only on your unforgiven feelings and then to actively forgive yourself and notice how you feel afterwards. It also involves noticing what ideas still get in the way of feeling forgiven.

WHAT'S IN THE WAY OF FORGIVING YOURSELF?

Before you start self-forgiveness work, it is important to find all the ideas you have that will get in your way.

Our culture is not supportive of forgiveness for ourselves or others. Forgiveness is seen as weak. I have given examples of this earlier in the chapter. Our grudge-holding is confusing because forgiveness is actually the central teaching of the Judeo-Christian ethic on which our culture is based. On Saturday, or Sunday, we hear about the importance of forgiveness. The most holy holiday for Jews is Yom Kippur, the day all is forgiven. The central teachings of the Sermon on the Mount include meekness, mercy, and peacemaking. The Lord's prayer includes the words, "...forgive us our trespasses as we forgive those who trespass against us." If these teachings are at the heart of our culture why are we so unforgiving of ourselves and others? We are clearly very confused when it comes to forgiveness.

A more personal barrier to forgiveness is the continual need for self-punishment. If you were raised in a family where there was a lot of criticism, you have probably learned to internalize the criticism. Now you don't need your judgmental parent telling you how rotten you are, you carry that voice inside your head. If you try to forgive yourself, the critical voice sings out loud and clear that you are bad or wrong and not entitled to forgiveness. The critical voice may accuse you of being self-indulgent, lazy, and unworthy of forgiveness. It will restate again and again how unforgivable you really are. If you find this happening while you are working on self-forgiveness, go back to Chapter Six, *Depression and Anger*, and read the section on cognitive therapy. Use the thought-stopping exercises to silence your critical voice and replace it with more humane, gentle, and realistic messages.

You may feel that you don't have time every day to devote to self-forgiveness. No matter how busy you are, no matter how many responsibilities you have, you can take fifteen minutes a day to heal yourself. You are already spending this time in self-flagellation and self-punishment, it's just in seconds and moments throughout your day. When you make the commitment to yourself to work on self-forgiveness in one fifteen minute block of time, you will find that you are not getting as caught in self-punishing moments and minutes during the rest of the day.

If you are not particularly religious, self-forgiveness may sound like a religious practice to you and you may resist it for that reason. Every religious tradition rests heavily on forgiveness (at least in principle), but forgiveness is also a psychological experience and doesn't need any spiritual framework around it. Unfortunately, because there is confusion about forgiveness and spirituality, there is very little psychological research or writing on this subject.[1] Don't let that stop you from doing this essential self-healing work. If you were raised in a faith that you have left, forgiveness may sound like something you had rammed down your throat and you don't want to be reminded about it now. Back then you may have understood that forgiveness was a one-time act, rather than a process, and that you had to do it on command. So you said, "I forgive my little brother for ruining my favorite toy," but you were thinking, "and I'm going to rip his ears off next time my parents aren't looking." Of course, this isn't forgiveness, and you knew in your heart that you were not only bad for not being able to forgive, you were also a liar. This isn't the process I'm suggesting you practice with now.

THE STEPS THAT COME BEFORE SELF-FORGIVENESS

The first thing you must do to forgive yourself for something is be aware of the feelings that need forgiveness. These can be about having done harm to another or yourself, feeling flawed to the core, or feeling stuck in anger. If you are struggling with a sense of having done harm after an abortion, it can be a feeling of having harmed the fetus or yourself physically. It can be a sense of spiritual or emotional harm to yourself, the fetus, your partner, or your relationship with whatever is most essential to you. It may be guilt from something in your past that has been stirred up by the anxiety of the abortion. It doesn't matter whom or what you feel you've hurt, just knowing that you feel this way is the beginning of the process. Feelings of shame and anger are the same; you have to acknowledge these painful feelings before you can forgive yourself or others, and move away from them.

For some women, but not all, the next step is talking about the abortion with someone else. Chapter Nine was about how to find a safe person to talk to, and how to prepare for the talk. If your abortion wasn't a secret, this step may not be as important to you in getting ready to forgive yourself, but you should still think about whether there are any unsaid things that are separating you from yourself or the people you care about most.

The third step is to do the grieving necessary for letting go. Grieving lets you learn deep lessons from the painful situation you have been in. If nothing else, you may need to grieve not being who you want to be, or thought you were. You may just be grieving your one-time inability to protect yourself from an unwanted pregnancy. If you feel you are not finished with grieving, go back and read Chapter Four again.

SELF-FORGIVENESS PRACTICE

Pick a time of day when you will usually be able to have fifteen minutes all to yourself. Turn your phone off. Make sure you will have no interruptions. Read the meditation below or make up your own meditation. Make sure that your meditation is truly forgiving and doesn't contain any subtle attacks on yourself. Then sit down, close your eyes and get comfortable. Notice anywhere in your body you may be holding tension and imagine your breath flowing into that area and loosening the tightness. Imagine the tension flowing out of your body with your out-breath.

When you are calm and relaxed, gently open your eyes and slowly read the meditation. Read one line at a time and then stop and close your eyes. Say that line over several times. Pause on each word and pay attention to the meaning of that word. Don't rush through this to get to the "important parts," or to the end. Read the next line. Close your eyes again and really listen to each word. Do this until you are finished with the meditation.[2]

Then take a few minutes, and keeping your eyes closed, imagine how it would feel to really believe the words you have just repeated to yourself. How would the feelings in your body change if you could really believe in your own forgiveness? How would your thoughts about yourself change? How would your heart change?

Notice any negative self-talk that comes along. Use the thought-stopping and replacement techniques you learned in Chapter Six to change your self-talk into a gentler, more realistic and more humane message.

You may feel a little lighter, a little more kind to yourself, but you will probably have to repeat this exercise many times before you realize that you have actually forgiven yourself.

FORGIVENESS MEDITATION

May I forgive myself for all acts of harm
I have done to myself,
either on purpose or by accident,
whether conscious or unconscious,
because I recognize
that I was acting out of my own
ignorance, confusion, and unskillfulness.

May I forgive myself for all acts of harm
I have done to others,
either on purpose or by accident,
whether conscious or unconscious,
because I recognize
that I was acting out of my own
ignorance, confusion, and unskillfulness.

You can be more specific and put the names of those you feel you have harmed into the meditation, or name the acts of harm you are working on forgiving yourself for.

THE STEPS THAT COME AFTER SELF-FORGIVENESS

After you have worked with self-forgiveness for a while, you may want to add a resolution not to repeat the action that you feel caused you or another harm. Be very careful as you think about this. Many women who are struggling after an abortion immediately resolve that they will never have another abortion. If they get pregnant again under difficult circumstances, they feel doubly bad about having a second abortion. The problem is in making a resolution before doing all the other work that has to be done (grieving, forgiveness), and in making the resolution too big.

If you have already resolved never to have another abortion, think carefully about what you would really do if you were raped, or if you accidentally got pregnant while taking a medication that was harmful to the fetus, or while you were working with toxic chemicals.

If you feel the need to make a resolution, think about the whole pregnancy experience in small pieces. Perhaps your resolution needs to be about not drinking on a first date alone with a man you don't know very well. Maybe your resolution needs to be about committing yourself to getting excellent reproductive health care and using your method of birth control consistently and correctly. Resolving to talk to your partner or a close friend or therapist before you make a decision about another unplanned pregnancy may be much more realistic than resolving never to have another abortion. Your resolution could be about a long-ago event that the anxiety of the abortion stirred up for you. In the future, if you find you haven't been able to stick to your resolution, it is not an indication that you're bad. It just suggests that you need more awareness of what motivates you. Finding a good therapist to help you investigate what's stopping you from sticking to your resolution can be helpful.

You may never feel the need to make any resolution about future pregnancies. This doesn't mean you're avoiding anything or you're not willing to do the work necessary to heal. Your experience is unique. As long as you are willing to be as honest as possible with yourself, you can create the healing that suits you best.

If you feel you have harmed someone else, you may feel the need to apologize to them and ask for their forgiveness. You may not feel this way at all, or you may want to, but not feel able to do this part of forgiveness work yet. Don't pressure or push yourself into anything that feels too uncomfortable. Remember that forgiveness is a process and not a one-time act and that the process can take as long as you need it to.

If you decide to apologize, write out what you intend to say first and practice it several times in your imagination before you talk to the person involved. If you feel you need to apologize to the fetus or baby and ask for its forgiveness, you can write out what you would say, and read it to yourself. Let yourself imagine that the baby hears and understands your apology, and forgives you. You can also apologize to someone you feel you hurt in the past by writing them a letter and imagining their response. If you are sure that sending the letter will not hurt this person, or that they will not hurt you as a result of receiving the letter, you can send it to them.

If you have been angry with someone else and you want to work on forgiving them, practice the forgiveness meditation on page 148 but read Note 2 on page 175 for how to turn it into a forgiveness-of-others meditation. At some point you may want to tell them you've forgiven them, but don't rush into this or push yourself to say you've forgiven them before you really have.

ATONEMENT

WHAT ATONEMENT IS NOT

Atonement is not about punishment, self-punishment or self abuse. Usually when you hear the word atonement it is in the same sentence as "sin." It may bring to mind having to do penance in church when you were young: someone telling you how many prayers to say in order to recognize the seriousness of your "sin" and then be forgiven for it. You may be thinking that atonement sounds like a good idea if you haven't suffered enough for having had the abortion. Atonement is not about making sure you suffer "enough," it is about *ending* your suffering.

WHAT ATONEMENT IS

Atonement is a word created two hundred years ago.[3] It is made from "at-one-ment," and it refers to actions you can take after you have done something you regret, which put you right ("at one") with what is most essential to your well-being. When you feel "at one," you *stop* hurting about your past actions. Acts of atonement let you feel more in harmony with yourself, or with God, nature, your family, friends or partner.

Many women who are healing from post-abortion distress don't feel the need for atoning actions. This section is here for those women who do. If this doesn't sound like something important to you now, read this section anyway because these ideas may be helpful later in working through your post-abortion distress, or they may become important in another life situation in the future.

Atonement involves restitution. Restitution means "paying back." This concept may make sense to you in your current situation or it may not. Some people working on forgiveness feel unfinished until they have made some restitution to the person they have injured. If you feel this way, first pay close attention to the desire to "pay back" in some way. Make sure it is about putting yourself right with the other person, or God, or nature. Make sure it is not about self-punishment or giving someone else, who you know will be punishing, the opportunity to hurt you.

If it is clear to you that your "payment" is not about continuing to hurt yourself, then make a list of all the things you imagine would let you feel "out of debt." For you to feel that you have "paid back," the work you do must involve some degree of effort or difficulty to feel valid. Most of my clients who have wanted to atone for an aspect of their abortion experience find that volunteer work has made the most sense to them. They are giving their work for free to people who need it. They are "paying back" to their community. If this makes sense to you, pick an agency that is interesting to you. It should be about an issue you feel strongly about, and it doesn't need to have anything to do with pregnancy, children, abortion, or adoption. Set a time limit on your volunteer work; don't let it drag on forever because this goes against the idea that you can be finished with your atonement and free from your distress. Most agencies have a minimum time commitment they want you to make, and you don't have to keep volunteering past that time unless you really want to.

Other clients who have felt the need to atone find that talking to someone they feel they have injured in the process of having the abortion feels like "paying back." Reread Chapter Nine, *Talking About It*, if this feels right for you. Make sure you are not motivated by a need to be punished any more.

Many religions have specific atonement rituals. The next section will look briefly at these.

RITUAL

WHAT RITUAL IS NOT

Ritual is not about doing the same action over and over without thinking about it. Many people become dissatisfied with their religion, their job, or their marriage because of the "ritualistic" quality to it: just the same empty words or gestures repeated meaninglessly every day or every weekend. Rituals do not have to be something you've been taught to do only in certain situations, like church or synagogue. Rituals don't have to have any religious significance for you at all.

WHAT RITUAL IS

When you work on changing your feelings about yourself and others, you change inside, psychologically or spiritually. You may also change inside without working on it at all, it can just happen. Rituals are actions you take in the outer world that show you or others how you've changed on the inside. One example of how ritual is an outer expression of an inner change is marriage. You have already changed (fallen in love with someone) and have decided you want to spend the rest of your life with that person; the marriage ritual just puts those internal changes out there for all the world to see. Not all rituals have to be as public as marriage though.

Performing a ritual for yourself, or with one other person, can deepen your understanding of the changes you have gone through. Women often find that including someone else makes the experience of doing a ritual more meaningful, because it demonstrates the "reconnected-to-others" quality of healing. If you can safely and comfortably include someone involved in your pregnancy and abortion, it can make the ritual even more important to your healing.

The whole idea of ritual may seem foreign to you. This makes sense because we live in a culture that doesn't have a lot of ritual observances. In many parts of the world there are rituals to make public the internal changes of puberty, or the deep grief following the death of someone well loved. Some American sub-cultures still have these kinds of rituals, but most often these major life transitions go by without any significant way of noting them.[4] You may not feel any need to perform a ritual to heal from your post-abortion distress. Like the ideas about atonement, these suggestions are here to use if they feel right to you, or to ignore if they don't make sense to you.

If you are not religious, you will need to create your own ritual. You can use elements of the rituals you may have learned as a child at church or you can take parts of rituals you have heard about and incorporate them into your own ritual.

If you are religious, one place to start looking for meaningful ritual is in your current faith. Does the church you go to or the religion you profess, have specific rituals for atonement, healing, and cleansing? If so, would doing one of these rituals feel right to you now? Sometimes, the rituals from your childhood religion may have more meaning for you than your current faith. Choose whatever mix of these rituals has the most meaning for you now.

There are four kinds of rituals that some of my clients have used or created and described to me. The first are rituals that demonstrate your sense of reconnection with whatever is most essential in your life. Jill, the woman in Chapter Three who wanted to bury the fetus under a tree in the woods, was doing a ritual of reconnection. Placing the fetus out in nature was her way of recognizing that it was part of the "wholeness" of life, even though she couldn't carry it to term. For Catholic women, receiving Eucharist is this same kind of connection-affirming ritual; it says that through forgiveness, you are always connected to God. Many other Christian denominations perform communion in various forms. Communion is about remembering your connection to the Essential. Some women plant a tree or garden to remember their connection to the life around them. This is a good example of a ritual of atonement because having planted the garden, you have to put effort into maintaining it.

If the post-abortion work you have been doing has been about grieving, then rituals which have to do with marking the passage of grief may be helpful to you. Lighting candles on the anniversary of your abortion, or the date you would have delivered if you hadn't had the abortion, can be very helpful in letting you note and pass these landmarks rather than staying stuck in the grief.

You may be feeling that the work you have done while reading this book has helped you and that you are feeling less distressed and overwhelmed. You may be feeling lighter and "cleaner" than you have in a long time. A third kind of ritual that can make this inner reality more solid for you is a ritual bath. Make time for yourself alone and create a pleasant environment with candles and incense. As you bathe, remember all the things that you felt stuck in that have now washed away.

The last kind of ritual is about letting go.

Vivian and I had worked for several months on the grief and guilt she had experienced after her second abortion. During one session, she told me that she wasn't holding on any more to the ideas about herself as bad or cruel that she had labeled herself with after the abortion. She also noticed that she wasn't thinking about the pregnancy all the time as she had been at the beginning of therapy and that it wasn't the focus of her life anymore.

The next week she brought in her "Letting Go" box. It was a shoe box that she had colored with crayons and pasted with pictures and words she had cut from magazines. Some of the words were pro-choice and anti-choice slogans. Some were about babies and some were the words that were the heart of her negative self-talk about the abortion. Inside the box she had placed the proof-of-pregnancy she had received when she first had her pregnancy test, and the receipt and other paperwork from her abortion. She felt relieved to have let go of the painful feelings attached to these words and objects. She said she was going to explain the box to her boyfriend. If he had anything he felt he had let go of about the abortion she was going to invite him to put it into the box and then she planned to go to the beach and burn it.

Self-forgiveness is the absolute heart of much of post-abortion healing. Even if it seems awkward at first, work with a forgiveness meditation for as long as you need to. Forgiving yourself or others won't happen overnight, but it can happen if you commit yourself to doing forgiveness work every day.

Atonement and ritual are ideas that are helpful to some women as they heal but may not be important to everyone. Use the parts of this chapter that really speak to your heart, and trust yourself enough to know what doesn't work for you, and ignore it.

11

HEALING INTO THE REST OF YOUR LIFE

Post-abortion distress is not a syndrome that each woman experiences just like the next woman. By now you have understood that *your* post-abortion distress is uniquely yours, and that the way to heal yourself is completely personal. Often, as you have discovered, post-abortion distress is really about other, long-buried issues in your life. No matter how painful or difficult these old feelings are, it is important to keep in mind that the pain you experience really can be healed. Other self-help books may be able to take you further on your healing journey. Some of these books are listed in the *Further Reading* section at the end of this book.

If you have done the exercises in this book, you have learned several useful skills for working with any distress you may still have. You've learned that your imagination is a powerful tool. You learned to use your imagination by doing the imagery exercise in Chapter Four, *Grief*, to discover more about what is going on inside you. In Chapter Six, *Depression and Anger*, you learned the skill of thought-stopping and replacing negative self-talk with more realistic and gentle words. Self-forgiveness, the heart of the healing in this book, was explained in Chapter Ten along with atonement and ritual. Each of these practices can add to the depth of relief you experience by working in a committed way on your own healing. Finally, Chapter Nine, *Talking About It*, contained suggestions for how to find someone to talk to about your abortion.

Possibly the most important thing you've learned from this book is that any crisis can be the motivator for dramatic life changes. Even something as dark as grief for the fetus or baby can open doors into parts of yourself about which you were unaware. The gift of grieving fully can be a complete re-evaluation of your values and goals: no small reward for the hard work you've done.

The insights you've gained in working through this book will help you in other areas of your life. If you have discovered that you are prone to depression, you now have information to get the help you need. If you have a new understanding of how you are imprisoned by shame, you can start to do the work that will liberate you from this terrible emotion. If you learned that it was important for you to talk to someone about your feelings, you can always draw on supportive people to help you through whatever life throws your way.

If you are still troubled by the feelings that lead you to read this book in the first place, you should seek professional counseling. Self help books and exercises can assist many, but not all people. It doesn't mean you're more troubled than someone who is helped by this book, or that you haven't tried hard enough to heal. Each woman is different and her road to healing from post-abortion distress will be unique.

This book has probably been hard to work your way through. It takes great courage to look deeply into painful and troubling parts of yourself. Two of the realistic, gentle and humane things you can say to yourself from now on when you are fighting against negative self-talk, are that you are brave for investigating your post-abortion distress, and that you are adventurous for being open to the positive transformation that comes from such deep investigation.

APPENDIX: HOW PARENTS FEEL

I have never had a client who was the parent of a daughter who had had an abortion or a son who had been involved in an abortion. I've never seen anything written anywhere about how these involved parents might feel. In talking to friends about writing this book, two people volunteered that their kids had had abortions which had left them feeling hurt, angry or confused. This chapter just contains two interviews. The first one is with a sixty-two year-old woman named Dot talking about her daughters' abortions.

"Joan is now 35, and when she was nineteen she was going with this guy in a pretty serious relationship....and they came to visit and she said she was pregnant and said, 'I don't know if I want to have this baby.' Her boyfriend wanted her to have the baby but he was already fooling around on her and she knew he wouldn't be good parent material. She asked me what I thought. At that time I was really unformed in my opinion about abortion and it was clear that she wanted direction from me. I didn't give it to her, I just said, 'You have to do what you want to do, what you think is right.' She said 'I know I don't want to be a single mother.' She was waitressing at the time and said, 'I see other single moms schlepping their kids to daycare at seven A.M. and living off tips.' So she went back to Santa Ana and had the abortion. I didn't have much in the way of feelings about it at the time. I had only left the Catholic Church four years before, and was still sort of in rebellion to the Church, so I guess at that time I was on the pro side of abortion. It was perfectly OK in my mind and I didn't have any emotional fallout. She had the abortion in another county so I wasn't with her.

"Then my second daughter, Meg, also got pregnant at age nineteen. She was not in a very serious relationship, just sort of friends. She came home and told us she was pregnant. By then (four years after Joan's) I was beginning to feel like this is a creation, not necessarily a life, but it has eye color, and I began thinking of the fetus more as a reality, and I toyed with the idea at the time that maybe she should have it and Greg and I could raise it. But she would not have gone along with it. We had a brief discussion about it but she wouldn't have been able to give it up. Also, it was totally unrealistic for us to think about raising the child. I'd have a ten year old now. At that time our family was barely out of the nest. The youngest was still at home. So I went with her to the abortion. I was with her. It was a pretty simple process; I think she had a few cramps. I numbed myself out to the whole thing; it was like standing by at a tooth extraction. The doctor gave her post-operative instructions. We drove home not talking about it. At that time I began to feel... I knew then that I could never have an abortion. I don't believe at all that it should be criminalized. Not at all. It's taken me almost 15 years to figure out that I don't believe in it, but I would never say it's really wrong for someone else to do it because I could never stand in their shoes. I just know it is not right for me.

"The last time Joan got pregnant with the baby that she had, she was separated from her husband and back with the love of her life and she got pregnant immediately. It was terrible timing, they hadn't lived together, they hardly knew each other, it had been a forbidden romance for years, and here she was pregnant by this guy who she really didn't know very well and she said, 'I'm going to have this baby,' and I said 'OK.' But the timing was such a mistake, and I said to her, 'Why are you having this baby?' and she said, 'Because I had another abortion after my first one and I knew I couldn't do it a third time so I have to have this baby.'

"Neither of them have expressed their *feelings* about their abortions with me. It was sort of interesting that they both told us that they were going to have abortions, and would we support or approve of, or whatever they were asking from us, but I don't know how in touch with their feelings about their abortions they are.

"What changed my feelings between Joan's abortion and Meg's? A lot of time, and just listening to the national discussion and getting clearer about...... When I got pregnant with Eve, I was thirty-two years old and had had five children, and this was sixteen months after my fifth child. I was very depressed—very depressed. I just felt my life was over. I just laid around and cried, and cried, and cried, for at least 3 weeks. Greg went into serious rebellion and rejection of me and the pregnancy. It was just terrible. I thought......wondered, if I could have an abortion, that's as close as I came to it. But in retrospect, I think that's probably been the biggest reason my feelings have changed, because that child, Eve, has been the evidence of the life I conceived. And she's the most gifted child, the most intelligent of the children. I don't know, I do sort of believe what the pro-birth (I don't call them pro-life) people say about...... not that it's a person...... but that there's something there right from the beginning. I just wouldn't have the nerve to have had an abortion. So having thought about it and not done it, and having seen her now at twenty-eight, I just realize that I couldn't cut that off. But that's just for me. If I had a twelve year old daughter who was raped and got pregnant, I'd probably encourage her to have an abortion.

"I have regret that those babies weren't allowed to live. Not that Joan and Meg didn't raise them, because that would have really been hard. I think this is my Catholic guilt, that somehow we couldn't take those lives on, couldn't allow them to be, couldn't absorb them into our families and just sort of say, 'Yes.' The regret isn't about grandchildren, it's about those lives that weren't allowed. I don't think of it as a person. Especially since I have so many grandchildren, eight of my own and two step-grandchildren. I don't think of them as grandchildren, and I'd be interested really... this conversation makes me wonder how Joan thinks about her abortion. What she went through and how she felt. She's not shared that with me and she didn't tell me about the second abortion until I really questioned her about the wisdom of having this baby, and when she explained it to me I thought, 'Oh, yeah, it makes sense.' And she's thrilled with this baby and so is her husband so it's... I don't know if the marriage is going to work but she's glad she's had this baby. That's another thing, by rights, she shouldn't have had this baby and yet this baby is just so adorable. My God, she's the cutest thing you ever saw. That's what informs me, you know, is that one little conception turns into a human being. I don't know... there's no point in those early three months where it changes for me even though this baby-killer rhetoric drives me nuts. It's still.. it's not a life, it's a potential life for me and that's enough to make me believe that abortion's not right. But whatever a woman has to do for herself, she has to do. I don't say anything is wrong for everybody because I can't in good conscience say that things should only be the way I want them. That's one of the things I don't agree with the Catholic Church on.

"I also recall, Meg had one or two more abortions that she didn't want me to know about at the time. When I found out I felt annoyance about using abortion as a method of birth control. And in Meg's case that's probably what she did, I mean, she was kind of a careless person.

"When my son, Bill, who is now thirty-seven, when he first got married, they got pregnant and his wife had an abortion. I just remembered that! He didn't tell me how he felt about it. Neither one of them did, they're pretty private. But they did tell me that she wasn't ready for motherhood, and having now watched her mother their two children I can certainly see why she thought about it seriously. She's just a really giving person and has let the children almost bury her alive. I don't know, Bill never told me how he felt about that.

"I remember when I was in college it was common for girls to get pregnant so the guy would have to marry them. That was very common. That's how beyond the pale abortion was in my generation. I graduated college in 1954 and in the early fifties that was a common event—he had to marry her. I had girlfriends tell me 'I got pregnant so we'd have to get married cause he wouldn't commit.' And that's so far from where we are now.

"I'm glad I never had an abortion as hard as that sixth child made it for our family. We could have coped with four, but six was just beyond coping. And now, even though we're still working because we used up all our money on the kids, I know myself, that I would still be thinking about that life."

The next interview is from a forty-two year old woman named Chris who got married at nineteen because she was pregnant. When the son she had as a result of that pregnancy told her that his girlfriend was going to have an abortion, it stirred up many feelings for her.

"Abortion had just been made legal when I was a junior in college and thought I might be pregnant. I went to the doctor to confirm the pregnancy and he mentioned the option of abortion, but counseled me to marry my boyfriend if we loved each other, and to have the child. I was, and am still, a practicing Catholic, so abortion was not my choice for myself. When I told George about the pregnancy, his response was that we should get married. We got married and even though I was afraid of some aspects of the pregnancy and labor, I became very attached to the pregnancy and deeply appreciated the preciousness of the child I was carrying. If I had had an abortion I think that now I would regret it.

"Things were tough for us at first. I had to quit school and my mother was upset and fretted about how to tell my dad about the pregnancy, but they were both supportive and uncritical of my choice, which was a big relief.

"Bobby was aware from the time he could add and subtract that he was conceived before we were married. Because this was a known fact in the family, it freed us up to talk to him about dating, girlfriends, and the importance of using birth control. It was a subject we talked about quite a few times, and we felt that we had done a good job of informing Bobby about sexual issues and the difficulties that arise when you have an unplanned pregnancy.

"Bobby didn't start dating until he got out of high school. The girl he started to date seriously was someone George and I didn't like. I'm not sure if that made him want to see her more or what. She was three years younger than Bobby, and for her age, much more sexually advanced than other girls. And she was light years ahead of Bobby. When we would ask to make sure he was using contraception, he could come back with, 'What do you think I am, stupid?' It's a very hard age when kids become more independent. You've kind of lost the control you had of them when they were younger. He was in college but not doing well because he had an undiagnosed learning disability. He was living at home, but wanting to be more independent, so he spent a lot of time in his relationship with his girlfriend. I don't know how involved they were, I'm assuming it (sex) was this one night when they went to her junior prom. He told me that some of her friends had gotten a motel room to party in so no one would have to drive drunk. I'm not sure if they did that, but I found out later on that they ended up having their own room at a different hotel. I'm just assuming that this is when it happened.

"I think I found out that she was pregnant from a post-card from her to Bobby. She had gone on vacation with her parents after school was out, and the post-card she sent him had a reference to her pregnancy. I think he knew about it before she had left. I called him on it and he wanted to know how I knew, and I told him I had read it on the back of his post-card. He admitted that she was pregnant and said, 'Don't worry mom, we're going to take care of it.' And I asked, 'Well what does that mean?' He said that when his girlfriend got back from vacation they were going to go see a counselor and get an abortion. I asked if that was what he wanted and he said, 'Well, it's her decision and I'm OK with it.' I asked if they had considered the other alternatives. They weren't considering getting married and apparently she felt it would be too hard to have the child and then give it up. I felt that it might be easier now, but that later in life she might wish she had given it up for adoption. Maybe because I didn't like her much anyway, I didn't press the point about adoption though. Bobby is very politically oriented and was very pro-choice, so it wasn't really a surprise to me that this was the decision they had made.

"I felt that George and I had both failed. Bobby ended up doing exactly what we had tried to warn him about. I was angry at him at first. First of all that he hadn't come and told us about her pregnancy when he first knew about it—about the way I had to find out about it. But I'm sure he was afraid, and at that time I think we weren't communicating as well as we do now. I was angry that he would allow something like this to happen. I questioned him about using birth control and if she was having sex why wasn't she on the pill? He said they were using a condom but it broke. I don't know if he was lying to me or if that's the truth. I hope to think that he was telling the truth.

"Then I was angry about the decision they were making, but on the other hand...... I went through a whole series of angry feelings. I was very angry and irrational for a couple of weeks. I guess I was angry first of all at the fact that he ended up getting a girl pregnant when she was so young, and the fact that he had done exactly what we had warned him about. I feel like we had failed him. And I was also upset that they were getting an abortion. But in my mind I was also saying, 'This way, if she has an abortion, she will be saving me the embarrassment of having anyone know he had gotten a girl pregnant.' But at the same time I was feeling guilty that I felt this way and condoning her having the abortion. I didn't totally agree with her decision. Parts of me wanted for her to have this baby, but another part of me wanted to get this out of the way so I didn't have to deal with it any more. It was really hard. I'd be torn back and forth about it. I'd see commercials on TV or see a baby and I'd feel bad.

"I'm pro-choice because I do think, after thinking about this for over a year and talking to my sister about it and other people, I've come to the decision that the decision they did make was probably the best for them for the rest of their lives. She really was a very young girl in high school. She obviously did not want to have the baby. In the long run I guess she ended up making the right decision. I think it would have been different, they would have made a different decision, if it was someone Bobby was truly in love with, and a little bit older. They probably would have gone for the choice of getting married and keeping the baby or giving it up for adoption.

"In moments of extreme tension at the beginning when he told me they were going to have an abortion I think I said to him, 'What if I had done that with you?' It wasn't a nice thing to say, but at that time I was really angry. He had hurt me the worst possible way that you can hurt a mother. When you think of it being a person, that's when you get upset.

"In the beginning it was hard to be around little children if I was around Bobby at the same time. My mind would flash to, 'She would be having the baby about now.' I wasn't trying to, but I was keeping a calendar of the pregnancy in my head. A couple of times when I was in church, the grieving for the baby really hit me the hardest, especially with certain songs that we would sing or at a baptism. I wasn't angry any more, I was grieving for the unborn child who was never going to be there. Bobby is really good with little kids. He has younger cousins whom he is great with. When I would see Bobby play with my two year old nephew that would bring out the grief.

"Talking about this now brings up some more sadness and grieving, but I'm not angry anymore. I think I forgave Bobby when we were talking six months after the abortion, and he told me about being in the room and seeing the ultrasound, and he cried while he told me, and I realized how hard it had been for him and how bad he had felt. I felt connected to him again because I could understand his feelings, and I think that's when I stopped dwelling on the abortion."

What I like most about these interviews is that they are not cut-and-dried. Both of these women talk about having conflicting feelings, and about the struggle to guide their children through something that is not easy for them. They are painfully honest in their self-assessment.

If you are a parent who is troubled or confused by your child's abortion, read the rest of this book if you haven't already. If you are grieving, adapt and do some of the exercises in the chapter on grief. If you have been depressed, follow the advice in the chapter on depression. If your child's abortion has stirred up other old issues you have kept buried out of consciousness, get the help you need to work on those issues and finally let go of them. It's never too late. This chapter is here to let you know that you are not alone if you are confused, sad, angry or hurt, or stirred up by your child's abortion.

CHAPTER NOTES

1   WHY AM I FEELING SO BAD?

1. Belsey, 1976, p.5.
2. Lazarus, 1985, pp.141-150.
3. Henshaw, 1988, p.164.

3   GUILT

1. *The Facts of Life*, Harold Morowitz, p.159.
2. One place to start researching is with *The Facts of Life* by Morowitz (see above). Other places to find information are from the Allan Guttmacher Institute in New York and the Centers for Disease Control in Atlanta. You can also write to pro-life organizations. Keep some questions in mind when evaluating anyone's research: Was this a large enough study to draw any conclusions from? Have the results been replicated in other, similar studies? Was the research done under similar circumstances to mine? (In other words, a study done 25 years ago in Eastern Europe, where abortion prac-

tices are much different, is not a valid study from which to draw conclusions about abortion in America now.)

3. Hatcher, 1994, p. 484.

4 *GRIEF*

1. Franco, 1989, pp.151-154.

5 *SHAME*

1. Speckhard, 1992, pp. 95-119.

6 *DEPRESSION AND ANGER*

1. Deitz, 1991, pp.61-70.
2. Only 0.1 - 0.3% of abortions are incomplete and need to be repeated. (Hatcher, 1994, p. 483.)

10 *SELF-FORGIVENESS, ATONEMENT AND RITUAL*

1. Out of over 800,000 psychological articles from fifty countries in twenty-seven languages, referenced in PsycLit, the research tool used by people doing research on psychological subjects, only 127 mention the word forgiveness, and only 6 mention self-forgiveness.

2. The rest of this meditation is for working with forgiveness toward others and goes: "May I forgive those who have hurt me (you can put their name and how they hurt you in here), either on purpose or by accident, whether consciously or unconsciously, because I recognize they were acting from their own ignorance, confusion, and unskillfulness. If I am unable to forgive others at this time, may I forgive myself for not being able to forgive." A third aspect of forgiveness meditation is asking in your heart for the forgiveness of others and seeing what it would feel like to you to be forgiven. "May others forgive me for all acts of harm I have done to them, either on purpose or by accident, whether consciously or unconsciously, because they recognize that I was acting from my own ignorance, confusion, and unskillfulness." This is a Buddhist meditation.

3. John Wesley (1703-1791) was the founder of the Methodist Church and invented the word "atonement."

4. "Quinceniera" is the fifteenth birthday party for Mexican-American girls; it is a major coming of age (puberty) ritual. Observant Jews "sit Shiva" for eight days after the death of a family member. About a year later they put a headstone on the grave to end the official period of mourning.

FURTHER READING

4 GRIEF

How To Go on Living When Someone You Love Dies. Theresa Rando, New York: Bantam Books, 1991.

6 DEPRESSION AND ANGER

On The Edge of Darkness. Kathy Cronkite, New York: Doubleday, 1994.

Mind Over Mood. Dennis Greenberger, Ph.D., New York: The Guilford Press, 1995.

Listening to Prozac. Peter Kramer, New York: Viking Press, 1993.

8 SOMETIMES MEN HAVE TROUBLE WITH ABORTION TOO

Men and Abortion. Arthur Shostak, New York: Praeger Publishers, 1984.

10 SELF-FORGIVENESS, ATONEMENT, AND RITUAL

A Path With Heart. Jack Kornfield, New York, Bantam Books, 1993.

A Gradual Awakening. Stephen Levine, New York: Anchor Books, 1989.

WOMENS' EXPERIENCES OF ABORTION IN THEIR OWN VOICES

The Choices We Made. Angela Bonavoglia, New York: Random House, 1991.

Ambivalence of Abortion. Linda Bird Franke, New York, Random House, 1977

Bitter Fruit. Rita Townsend, Alameda: Hunter House, 1991.

ABORTION IN ANOTHER CULTURE

Liquid Life: Abortion and Buddhism in Japan. William LaFleur, Princeton: Princeton University Press, 1992.

BIBLIOGRAPHY

Adler, Nancy, *et al*, "Psychological Responses After Abortion." Science, v.248, April, 1990.

American Psychiatric Association, *Diagnostic and Statistical Manual of Mental Disorders, Fourth Edition*. Washington, D.C., 1994.

Belsey, E., "Psychological Consequences of Abortion." Family Planning Association Newsletter, v.60, April, 1976.

Deitz, Jeffrey, "The Psychodynamics and Psychotherapy of Depression: Contrasting the Self Psychological and the Classical Psychoanalytic Approaches." American Journal of Psychoanalysis, v.51, n.1, 1991.

Franco, Kathleen, *et al*, "Anniversary Reactions and Due Date Responses Following Abortion." Psychotherapy and Psychosomatics, v.52, n.1-3, 1989.

Hatcher, Robert A., *et al*, *Contraceptive Technology*. New York: Irvington Publishers, Inc., 1994.

Henshaw, S.K. , *et al*, "The Characteristics and Prior Contraceptive Use of U.S. Abortion Patients." Family Planning Perspectives, v.20, n.4, 1988.

Lazarus, A., "Psychiatric Sequelae of Legalized First Trimester Abortion." <u>Journal of Psychosomatic Obstetrics and Gynecology</u>, v.4, n.3, 1985.

Morowitz, Harold, *et al*, *The Facts of Life*. New York: Oxford University Press, 1992.

Speckhard, Anne, *et al*, "Postabortion Syndrome: An Emerging Public Health Concern." <u>Journal of Social Issues</u>, v.48 n.3, 1992.

IF YOU FIND ANY GRAMMATICAL OR
TYPOGRAPHICAL ERRORS IN THIS BOOK,
PLEASE BRING THEM TO THE ATTENTION OF
THE PUBLISHER:

PIMPERNEL PRESS
P.O. BOX 33110
SAN DIEGO, CA 92163-3110

Pimpernel Press
P.O. Box 33110, San Diego, CA 92163-3110
(619) 266-8089

Please send me _____ copies of *Peace After Abortion* at $9.95 each $ _____
                    If ordering from California, add 7¼% sales tax $ _____
                    or if ordering from San Diego, add 7¾% sales tax $ _____

Shipping and handling:
        (1-3 copies $2, 4-6 copies $3, More? Call for shipping charges) $ _____

                                                        Total $ _____

Name _____

Address _____

_____ Phone (___) _____